AYUWAT
JEARWATTANAKANOK

BIRDS OF
THAILAND

A PHOTOGRAPHIC GUIDE

H E L M
LONDON · OXFORD · NEW YORK · NEW DELHI · SYDNEY

HELM
Bloomsbury Publishing Plc
50 Bedford Square, London, WC1B 3DP, UK
29 Earlsfort Terrace, Dublin 2, Ireland

BLOOMSBURY, HELM and the Helm logo are trademarks
of Bloomsbury Publishing Plc

This edition published 2024

A catalogue record for this book is available from the British Library.

Library of Congress Cataloguing-in-Publication data has been applied for.

ISBN: 978-1-399-41471-5;
ePub: 978-1-399-41470-8; ePDF: 978-1-399-41473-9

2 4 6 8 10 9 7 5 3 1

Design by Rod Teasdale
Map by Julian Baker

Printed and bound in China by RR Donnelley
Asia Printing Solution Ltd, Dongguang, Guangdong

To find out more about our authors and books visit www.bloomsbury.com
and sign up for our newsletters

CONTENTS

INTRODUCTION

Situated in the centre of mainland South-east Asia, Thailand is home to more than 1,000 species of birds, many of which are shared with the surrounding countries (Myanmar, Laos, Cambodia and Malaysia). This photographic guide is aimed mainly at those who visit Thailand, or even its neighbouring countries, and would like to explore the rich and wonderful birdlife that the region has to offer. I also hope that the guide will spark some interest in local birds for those who live in the country.

While it is impossible to include every species found in Thailand within such a compact guidebook, here you will find 400 species that are most likely to be seen, along with some specialities that attract birders from all over the world. The description of each species includes size (body length from bill tip to tail tip), appearance, behaviour, and where to see it. These descriptions are kept as short and as simple as possible, highlighting the easiest way to identify the birds in question. The accompanying photos have been selected to show the largest suite of features useful for identifying each species.

I have selected the species to reflect the diversity of birds in every major region and habitat in Thailand, including common and widespread species such as Eurasian Tree Sparrow, Oriental Magpie-robin, Asian Koel and Great Myna, as well as scarce and more localised species such as Green-tailed Sunbird, Coral-billed Ground-cuckoo, Rhinoceros Hornbill and Spoon-billed Sandpiper. These species are present in all kinds of habitats in Thailand, ranging from high mountains, forests, wetlands, grasslands and urban areas, to coastal mudflats, salt pans and mangroves. Also included is a section on good sites for birdwatching. You will find most of the famous birdwatching hotspots in the country, along with a list of some of the species at each site. Please note that due to some species being rare and very localised, they are not all covered in the species account section which focuses on those most likely to be seen across the country.

I have followed the taxonomy and nomenclature used by the Clements Checklist which is also the default taxonomy on eBird, a widely used application for recording bird species. Keep in mind that bird taxonomy is always changing and for now there is no single recognised authority, so you may find different names for the same species, or species in this book that are not recognised by some other checklists.

You may also find birds that are not included in this book or photos of a particular species that don't quite represent the bird that you saw. I encourage you to also seek more information about birds in Thailand via other sources. Thailand has a large and growing community of birders. You might be surprised to find how much you can learn from both the online platforms and while bumping into other birders in the field.

I hope you enjoy birding in Thailand. Don't forget to be respectful of the birds and places that you visit. The welfare of nature must come first. Try to avoid disturbing birds or altering their habitats.

BIRD CONSERVATION

Thailand is rich in both bird diversity and habitats. Although only three species are endemic to the country, more than 1,000 species have been recorded and the number is still growing. The three endemic birds are White-eyed River Martin, Turquoise-throated Barbet and Rufous Limestone Babbler. However, Thailand has a decent number of species that are restricted in range to only few countries in mainland Southeast Asia, as well as birds from different biogeographical regions and migrants.

Mountain ranges in the north and west are extensions of the Sino-Himalayan region and these hold species that occur only at high elevations. The central region consists of vast floodplains that host many species of waterfowl and farmland birds. The northeastern region is bordered by the transnational Mekong River and is home to many globally and regionally threatened species such as Great Thick-knee, Mekong Wagtail and River Tern. Mudflats and salt pans around the Gulf of Thailand represent one of the most important sites for migratory shorebirds in the world, most notably for the globally threatened Spoon-billed Sandpiper and Nordmann's Greenshank. Lastly, the southern region forms part of the Sundaland biogeographic region and shares many species of birds with Malaysia and Indonesia.

Shorebirds survey at Pak Thale Nature Reserve.

Compared to other countries in the region, Thailand has a relatively large number of protected areas, including 131 national parks, 62 wildlife sanctuaries and 96 non-hunting areas. Some of the best-known protected areas include Doi Inthanon National Park, Khao Yai National Park, Kaeng Krachan National Park, Hala-Bala Wildlife Sanctuary, Huai Kha Khaeng Wildlife Sanctuary, Bueng Boraphet Non-hunting Area and Nong Bong Khai Non-hunting Area. However, the majority of these protected zones cover only hilly or mountainous areas while the vast lowlands are largely unprotected. Primary lowland forests are among the most threatened habitats in Thailand, followed by wetlands and coastal habitats. These are among the first areas to be converted into plantations and urban areas. Nearly 100 species of birds that rely on such habitats are considered nationally threatened and some have become extinct, such as Gurney's Pitta, Chestnut-necklaced Partridge, Yellow-crowned Woodpecker, White-shouldered Ibis and Giant Ibis.

While nearly every species of bird in Thailand is protected by law, illegal trade and hunting persist. In the south, where people like to keep birds in cages, many of the popular songbirds such as Red-whiskered Bulbul, White-rumped Shama, Chestnut-capped Thrush and several species of leafbirds are in serious decline. These species are caught and sold as pets for people to enjoy their sweet and complex songs. One species, the Straw-headed Bulbul, has been driven to extinction for this very reason. Hunting and the use of mist-nets for trapping still occurs throughout the country, especially in farmland and around aquaculture ponds where people employ the nets to protect their crops or intentionally catch birds that roost in large numbers, such as the globally threatened Yellow-breasted Bunting.

On the brighter side, the average Thai citizen has become more aware of environmental issues in recent years. Younger generations have shown more interest in birds and nature. Birdwatching and bird photography have quickly gained popularity among the public, and alternative conservation measures such as private nature reserves have been established and bird tourism is gaining traction. The establishment of Pak Thale Nature Reserve, one of the world's most important wintering sites for the Critically Endangered Spoon-billed Sandpiper, along with the reintroduction of Sarus Cranes in Buriram, and the increase in population of Green Peafowl and many large waterbirds are some of the most successful cases of bird conservation in Thailand. The more that people learn about birds and their surroundings, the more likely they will be to support nature conservation.

Key to the photos
All images depict an adult, unless otherwise stated. The key below explains the regularly used abbreviations.

Male – ♂	Juvenile – juv.	Breeding – br.
Female – ♀	First-winter – 1st-win.	Non-breeding – non-br.

MAP OF THE REGION

GOOD BIRDWATCHING SITES IN THAILAND

NORTH

Doi Inthanon National Park
18°35'20.8"N 98°29'12.6"E
The park includes the highest peak in Thailand at 2,565m above sea level. It is one of the most accessible and popular birdwatching sites. The well-paved road that leads up to the summit transits from dry deciduous forest in the foothills to lush cloud forest on the summit. Significant species that can be found include Green-tailed Sunbird, Himalayan Shortwing, Green Cochoa, Chestnut-tailed Minla, Dark-sided Thrush and Grey-sided Thrush.

Doi Inthanon National Park.

Doi Lang (west) aka Doi San Ju
20°04'25.7"N 99°05'50.2"E
The border road that stems off from Fang town is part of the Doi Pha Hom Pok National Park. The road which runs along the mountain ridge is one of the most popular birdwatching sites in Thailand, especially during winter. Mrs. Hume's Pheasant, Himalayan Cutia,

Spot-breasted Parrotbill, White-bellied Redstart and Hodgson's Frogmouth are among some of the rare birds that can be found regularly.

Doi Lang (west).

Doi Lang (east)
20°07'56.8"N 99°09'32.5"E
Unlike Doi Lang (west), the eastern part of the mountain is covered with moist montane evergreen forest. Several bird species only occur on the eastern side, such as Pygmy Flycatcher, Black-eared Shrike-babbler, Whiskered Yuhina, Brown-crowned Scimitar-babbler and Pale-billed Parrotbill. Due to the

Doi Lang (east).

extremely rough condition of the road, a four-wheel drive vehicle is required to access the best birding spots.

Doi Ang Khang
19°51'47.8"N 99°03'05.1"E
Located on the Thai/Myanmar border, Doi Angkhang is home to many range-restricted species such as Giant Nuthatch, Brown-breasted Bulbul, Crested Finchbill and Scarlet-faced Liocichla. Orchards and flower gardens within the Royal Project also offer lots of good birds during winter such as Mrs. Gould's Sunbird, Spot-winged Grosbeak and many species of thrushes.

Doi Ang Khang.

Doi Pha Hom Pok National Park
20°02'43.0"N 99°08'42.8"E
This park covers the second-highest peak in Thailand at 2,285m above sea level. The summit can be accessed only via a hiking trail starting at Kew Lom campsite. The summit area shares similar species with Doi Inthanon and Doi Lang, such as Chestnut-tailed Minla, Himalayan Cutia, Black-throated Bushtit, Hume's Treecreeper and Crimson-breasted Woodpecker.

Wat Tham Pha Plong Temple
19°24'12.8"N 98°55'16.6"E
The temple is one of the most popular birdwatching sites in Chiang Dao district.

Early morning around the parking area usually provides a good variety of birds such as Pin-tailed Green-pigeon, Blue-throated Barbet, Asian Fairy-bluebird, Black-hooded Oriole, Puff-throated Bulbul, Grey-eyed Bulbul and Scarlet Minivet. The stairway leading up to the pagoda is a good area to look for Streaked Wren-Babbler and Red-headed Trogon.

Muang Khong
19°23'14.5"N 98°42'43.6"E
The Mae Taeng River which runs through the small town of Muang Khong is the best place in Thailand to see the rare Crested Kingfisher. Several individuals can be found along the river, even near the main road. It is also one of the few breeding sites for Common Kingfisher in Thailand. Wire-tailed Swallow, Little Ringed Plover and Green Sandpiper are among other significant species. The forest before Muang Khong town is also a good area to look for Black-backed Forktail.

Muang Khong.

Nong Bong Khai Non-Hunting Area
20°15'40.6"N 100°02'48.2"E
Nong Bong Khai (Chiang Saen Lake) is one of the largest lakes in northern Thailand. It is also an important wintering site for many waterfowl. Indian Spot-billed Duck, Ferruginous Duck, Pheasant-tailed Jacana and Oriental Darter are

among the species that can be found regularly, while rarities such as Baer's Pochard, Falcated Duck and Mandarin Duck can also be seen during winter.

Wiang Nong Lom
20°13'52.3"N 100°00'53.1"E
The wetland area is an extension of Chiang Saen Lake. It is well known for supporting the largest harrier roost in Thailand. Several hundred harriers come to roost in this area every year between October and April. Pied Harrier is the most numerous species, followed by Eastern Marsh Harrier. Rarities that have been recorded include Hen Harrier, Western Marsh Harrier and Chinese Rubythroat.

Nam Kham Nature Reserve
20°17'16.5"N 100°03'26.4"E
One of the few private nature reserves in Thailand, the reserve covers a large area of reedbeds and ponds. Several hides have been constructed in the reedbed to facilitate observing the birds that visit waterholes during the dry season. The reserve is best known for bush and reed warblers during migration periods. Chestnut-crowned Bush Warbler, Jerdon's Bushchat, Baikal Bush Warbler, Siberian Rubythroat and Chestnut-capped Babbler are among the species that can be expected.

Doi Lo Paddies
18°29'29.4"N 98°49'33.2"E
This vast area of rice fields is one of the most-visited birdwatching sites in northern Thailand to see farmland birds. Many migratory species can be found during the winter months, including Black Kite, Greater Spotted Eagle, Booted Eagle, Siberian Rubythroat and Pallas's Grasshopper Warbler. Rarities such as Common Crane, Greylag Goose, Imperial Eagle, Bonelli's Eagle and Brown-cheeked Rail have also been recorded.

Ban Thi Paddies
18°39'01.1"N 99°08'45.2"E
This area of rice fields is another of the most important places in northern Thailand for migratory birds, especially birds of prey. Several rare species occur each winter, including Imperial Eagle, Steppe Eagle, Greater Spotted Eagle and Short-toed Snake-Eagle. Other species that can be found include Bluethroat, Siberian Rubythroat, Horsfield's Bushlark, Oriental Skylark and Red Avadavat.

Mae Ping National Park
17°33'40.1"N 98°52'36.5"E
Mae Ping supports the largest area of primary deciduous forest in northern Thailand. Many dry-forest specialties

Nam Kham Nature Reserve.

Mae Ping National Park.

such as White-rumped Falcon, Collared Falconet, Burmese Nuthatch, White-bellied Woodpecker and Black-headed Woodpecker can be found here. The road leading to Thung Kik Ranger Station is the most-visited route for birding in the park.

Thung Thalay Luang
17°03′03.1″N 99°47′34.6″E
The heart-shaped island in the middle of the lake is one of the most outstanding landscapes in Sukhothai. The island is one of the best places to see the local and declining subspecies of Long-tailed Shrike (*longicaudatus*). Freckle-breasted Woodpecker, Plain-backed Sparrow, Siamese Pied Starling and Vinous-breasted Starling are among some of the other interesting species that can be found at this site.

Si Satchanalai National Park
17°33′11.9″N 99°29′07.8″E
The park is one of the few places in Thailand where Blue-naped Pitta is found regularly. There are also many other species to be searched for, including Collared Babbler, Blue Pitta, Hainan Blue Flycatcher, Scaly-breasted Partridge, Common Hill Myna and Bay Woodpecker. The park also offers a pleasant campsite with forest trails and a hide for birdwatching at the waterhole during the dry season.

CENTRAL

Bueng Boraphet Non-Hunting Area
15°40′26.3″N 100°14′37.0″E
Bueng Boraphet is the largest freshwater lake in Thailand. It is the only place where the mysterious White-eyed River Martin has been recorded, albeit not for several decades. Many species of ducks can be found during winter, including the globally threatened Baer's Pochard. Large waterbirds such as Spot-billed Pelican, Painted Stork and Oriental Darter are also recorded regularly.

Bueng Boraphet Non-Hunting Area.

Wat Phra Phutthabat Noi Temple
14°39′06.3″N 100°58′43.8″E
The limestone mountains around the parking area for the temple represent one of the few places in the country where the endemic Rufous Limestone Babbler can be found regularly. The babblers are usually seen foraging in pairs or small flocks on the limestone and among the dense vegetation.

Wat Phra Phutthabat Noi Temple.

Pak Phli Paddies

14°05'49.8"N 101°16'21.5"E

The vast grassland and rice paddies at Pak Phli are home to hundreds of Black Kites during winter. Other significant species that can be found at this site include Greater Spotted Eagle, the now globally threatened Yellow-breasted Bunting, Striated Grassbird, Horsfield's Bushlark, Oriental Skylark and the local subspecies of Long-tailed Shrike.

Pathum Thani Rice Research Centre

14°00'45.3"N 100°43'39.4"E

Located on the north-eastern side of Bangkok, this large area of rice fields is one of the most convenient places to see farmland birds. Flocks of large waterbirds such as Asian Openbill, Painted Stork and Black-headed Ibis are nearly always present. Other notable species include Indochinese Roller, Red Avadavat, Greater Painted-snipe, Pheasant-tailed Jacana, Bronze-winged Jacana and Stork-billed Kingfisher.

Queen Sirikit Park

13°48'27.1"N 100°33'02.1"E

The complex of urban parks near Chatuchak offers the largest green space in Bangkok, with Queen Sirikit Park being the best area for birdwatching. It is possible to find nearly all of the common urban species here, and rarities have been recorded during migration. Spotted Owlet, Asian Barred Owlet, Collared Scops Owl, Small Minivet, Stork-billed Kingfisher and Indochinese Roller are some of the usual highlights, while rarities have included Fairy Pitta, Narcissus Flycatcher, Ruddy Kingfisher, Slaty-legged Crake and Brown-chested Jungle-flycatcher.

Benchakitti Park

13°43'46.8"N 100°33'18.5"E

Located right in the centre of Bangkok, this park offers a great opportunity for visitors who may not have much time for birdwatching. Unlike other parks in Bangkok, it was designed to include different types of habitats, from lawns with planted large trees, to marshes and reedbeds. Resident species such as Spotted Owlet, Coppersmith Barbet, Yellow-bellied Prinia, Stork-billed Kingfisher and Black-collared Starling can be found year-round, while winter migrants such as Black-browed Reed Warbler, Oriental Reed Warbler and Black-capped Kingfisher have also been recorded.

Phutthamonthon Park

13°46'48.9"N 100°19'08.6"E

Being further away from Bangkok city centre to the west, this park has a higher diversity of birds and habitats. Apart from the common resident and migratory species, rarities such as Indian Thick-Knee, Von Schrenck's Bittern, Large Blue Flycatcher and Fairy Pitta have also been observed.

Bang Pu Recreation Centre

13°30'54.1"N 100°39'15.6"E

The bridge that leads into the Gulf of Thailand at the recreation centre is one of the best places in Thailand to see migrant gulls and terns. The most numerous species is Brown-headed Gull but Black-headed Gull, Slender-billed Gull, Black-tailed Gull and Heuglin's Gull can also be seen in small numbers. The nearby mangrove also has large flocks of Black-tailed Godwits and many Black-capped Kingfishers visit every winter.

Khok Kham

13°30'46.0"N 100°21'01.4"E

Located close to Bangkok, Khok Kham is one of the most convenient sites to see the globally threatened Spoon-billed Sandpiper. Thousands of other shorebirds can be found roosting and foraging in the salt pans during winter, including Great Knot, Red Knot, Curlew Sandpiper and Tibetan Sand-Plover.

NORTH-EAST

Khao Yai National Park

14°26'20.8"N 101°22'19.6"E

Khao Yai was the first national park to be established in Thailand. The park is popular among naturalists and general tourists as it is only around a three-hour drive from Bangkok. Coral-billed Ground-cuckoo, Siamese Fireback, Banded Kingfisher, Great Hornbill and Brown Hornbill are among the most sought-after species by visiting birders. Apart from birds, the park also offers great opportunities to see other wildlife such as Asian Elephant, Sambar Deer, Golden Jackal and Dhole.

Khao Yai National Park.

Sakaerat Environmental Research Station

14°30'35.5"N 101°55'50.6"E

This research station is located in lowland dry evergreen forest and is one of the best places in Thailand to see Siamese Fireback. The firebacks in this area are habituated to humans and can be observed at close range. Other significant species that can be found here include Scaly-crowned Babbler, Banded Kingfisher, Orange-breasted Trogon and Brown Prinia.

Bueng Lahan

15°38'08.0"N 101°55'09.6"E

The lake is well known for its abundant water lilies that bloom during the dry season. It is also home to many resident and migratory birds such as the beautiful Pheasant-tailed Jacana, Oriental Darter, Little Grebe, Cotton Pygmy-goose, Glossy Ibis and Grey-headed Swamphen. Bueng Lahan is also one of the few sites where the country's near-endemic subspecies of Long-tailed Shrike can still be found regularly.

Bueng Lahan.

Nam Nao National Park

16°44'22.4"N 101°34'24.9"E

Situated among deciduous forest on a plateau, the park is one of the best birdwatching sites in the north-east.

Many species of woodpeckers can be found here, including White-bellied Woodpecker, Great Slaty Woodpecker and Grey-headed Woodpecker. Burmese Nuthatch, Brown Prinia, Collared Babbler, Red-billed Blue-magpie and Red-headed Trogon are among some of the other specialties in the area.

Phu Khieo Wildlife Sanctuary
16°23'12.4"N 101°34'12.1"E
The sanctuary is well known for its beautiful scenery, including reservoirs and grasslands inside the forest. It is the most accessible place to see the reintroduced White-winged Duck in Thailand.
Apart from the duck, it is also a good site to find many other forest species such as Siamese Fireback, Indochinese Cuckooshrike, Red-billed Blue-magpie, White-crested Laughingthrush and Black-and-buff Woodpecker.

Phu Khieo Wildlife Sanctuary.

Phu Suan Sai National Park
17°30'13.2"N 100°56'21.4"E
This park is the best place in Thailand to see the rare and range-restricted Short-tailed Parrotbill. Other highly localised species such as Rufous-throated Fulvetta and Blue-naped Pitta can also be found in the forest around the park's headquarters.

Phu Suan Sai National Park.

Huai Chorakhe Mak Reservoir
14°54'12.0"N 103°01'01.2"E
The reservoir is well known for its reintroduced population of Sarus Crane, a species that was formerly adjudged to be extinct in the wild in Thailand. Nowadays, the cranes can be found regularly and in increasing numbers around the reservoir. Many other waterbirds can also be found at this site, including Painted Stork, Oriental Darter, Grey-headed Swamphen and Cotton Pygmy-goose.

Huai Chorakhe Mak Reservoir.

Khong Chiam Rapids
15°23'49.6"N 105°32'42.0"E
River rapids along the Mekong River in Khong Chiam, especially around Ban Ta Mui village, represent probably the best place in Thailand to see some of the Mekong specialties, including Mekong

Wagtail, Great Thick-Knee, Small Pratincole, Wire-tailed Swallow and even River Tern. It is recommended to visit during winter and the dry season when the water level is not too high. Local boats are available for birding along the rapids.

EAST

Ko Man Nai
12°36'43.3"N 101°41'18.4"E
A small island located on the eastern side of the Gulf of Thailand, this is one of the most important stopover sites for migratory landbirds in spring. Many globally Threatened and Near Threatened species have been recorded during spring migration, such as Fairy Pitta, Japanese Paradise-flycatcher and Brown-chested Jungle-flycatcher. The best period to visit the island is between March and April.

Ko Man Nai.

Prasae Estuary
12°41'46.9"N 101°42'21.6"E
The estuary is one of the few places in Thailand where the globally endangered Nordmann's Greenshank can be found regularly during winter. Apart from the greenshank, the mudflats and sandbar also host numerous other species of waders such as Ruddy Turnstone, Terek Sandpiper, Bar-tailed Godwit, Eurasian Curlew and Whimbrel.

WEST

Taksin Maharat National Park
16°46'48.9"N 98°55'43.2"E
This park offers quiet and comfortable campsites with great scenery including pine forest and montane evergreen forest. Many range-restricted species can be found rather easily, including Ayeyarwady Bulbul, Olive Bulbul, White-throated Bulbul, Slender-billed Oriole and Kalij Pheasant.

Taksin Maharat National Park.

Mae Moei National Park
17°28'53.7"N 98°04'28.0"E
Located at the border between Thailand and Myanmar, the park is home to several scarce and very localised species. It is the only place in Thailand where it is possible to find the Rufous-headed Parrotbill. Other significant species include Pale-billed Parrotbill, Collared Babbler, Red-billed Scimitar-babbler, White-throated Bulbul and Olive Bulbul.

Mae Wong National Park
16°06'00.4"N 99°06'27.7"E
This park is one of the most-visited birdwatching hotspots in western

Thailand. The Chong Yen campsite is the most accessible place in Thailand to see the globally threatened Rufous-necked Hornbill. Other significant species that can be found around the campsite include Burmese Yuhina, Brown-crowned Scimitar-babbler, Spot-necked Babbler, White-necked Laughingthrush, Rufous-throated Partridge, Kalij Pheasant and Grey Peacock-Pheasant.

Huai Kha Khaeng Wildlife Sanctuary
15°36′30.1″N 99°19′05.5″E
The sanctuary is well known for its rich wildlife. Many species characteristic of dry deciduous forest can be found here including White-rumped Falcon, Collared Falconet, White-bellied Woodpecker, Yellow-footed Green-pigeon and Green Peafowl. Large mammals such as Banteng, Eld's Deer, Asian Elephant and even Tiger can also be found.

Hup Pa Tat
15°22′38.2″N 99°37′51.9″E
This large sinkhole surrounded by limestone karst is the best place to see the range-restricted Variable Limestone Babbler. As well as Kalij Pheasant, the mammals Indochinese Grey Langur and Northern Serow are some of the other significant species also found here.

Hup Pa Tat.

Pak Thale Nature Reserve
13°09′00.8″N 100°03′41.4″E
Privately managed by the Bird Conservation Society of Thailand (BCST), the reserve is home to more than 10,000 shorebirds each winter. It is one of the best places in the world to see the globally threatened Spoon-billed Sandpiper, Nordmann's Greenshank and Great Knot. The area mainly comprises a series of salt pans with adjacent mudflats exposed at low tide. Red-necked Stint, Curlew Sandpiper, Broad-billed Sandpiper, Eurasian Curlew and Tibetan Sand-Plover are among some of the most abundant species.

Pak Thale Nature Reserve.

Laem Phak Bia
13°02′26.2″N 100°05′34.0″E
Located not too far from Pak Thale, Laem Phak Bia is another important site for shorebirds in Thailand. Most of the species are shared between the two sites, but the Laem Phak Bia sandspit is one of the few places in the country where Malaysian Plover and White-faced Plover can be found regularly.

Kaeng Krachan National Park
12°47′57.4″N 99°27′15.7″E
The biggest national park in Thailand, Kaeng Krachan supports some of the

largest numbers of species recorded in any protected area. The park is truly unique, with an equal mix of birds from northern and southern regions of the country. It is the best place in Thailand to see the rare Ratchet-tailed Treepie. Other magnets for birders include Ferruginous Partridge, White-fronted Scops Owl, Eared Pitta and many species of broadbills and kingfishers. There are many private bird hides around the park where birds can be seen and photographed at close range.

Khao Sam Roi Yot
12°14'38.5"N 99°55'56.9"E
A large wetland surrounded by limestone mountains, Khao Sam Roi Yot is one of the most scenic birdwatching sites. It is home to a wide variety of species of waterbirds such as Pheasant-tailed Jacana, Bronze-winged Jacana, Pied Kingfisher, Indian Cormorant and Painted Stork. The rare and globally threatened Manchurian Reed Warbler can also be encountered during winter.

SOUTH

Khao Dinsor
10°38'00.1"N 99°17'11.2"E
This mountain is one of the best places in Asia to observe raptor migration

in autumn. Hundreds to thousands of raptors can be seen flying over the mountain daily between mid-September and the end of October. Chinese Sparrowhawk, Japanese Sparrowhawk, Oriental Honey-buzzard, Grey-faced Buzzard and Black Baza are some of the most abundant species.

Krung Ching Waterfall
08°43'26.8"N 99°40'04.0"E
A designated ranger station within Khao Luang National Park, the entrance to the waterfall is one of the most visited birdwatching sites in southern Thailand. Many lowland species can be found along the trail to the waterfall, including Malayan Banded Pitta, Green Broadbill, Rufous-collared Kingfisher, White-crowned Hornbill, Wallace's Hawk-Eagle and Diard's Trogon.

Sri Phang Nga National Park
08°59'54.8"N 98°27'27.6"E
The park is well known for its diversity of lowland forest birds and is among the best places to see Gould's Frogmouth, Malayan Banded Pitta and Malaysian Blue-banded Kingfisher. In winter, the rare and little-known Large Blue Flycatcher is also regularly found here.

Ao Phang Nga National Park
08°24'02.2"N 98°30'38.7"E
The mangrove forest around the park's headquarters is one of the best places to see mangrove species such Mangrove Pitta, Brown-winged Kingfisher, Ruddy Kingfisher and White-chested Babbler. Other scarce and localised birds that can be found include Chestnut-bellied Malkoha, Streak-breasted Woodpecker and Rufous-bellied Swallow.

Khao Dinsor.

Laem Pakarang
08°44'10.3"N 98°13'21.0"E
The Thai name literally means 'Coral Cape' as the cape is mostly formed of small broken corals. Every year during the winter months, the area hosts hundreds of migratory waders such as Ruddy Turnstone, Terek Sandpiper, Tibetan Sand-Plover, Bar-tailed Godwit and Grey-tailed Tattler. The scarce resident Malaysian Plover can also be found at this site.

Laem Pakarang.

Mu Ko Surin National Park
09°26'10.9"N 97°52'01.5"E
This national park is located in the northern Andaman Sea. It is well known for its beautiful sandy beaches and coral reefs. Many rare and nationally threatened species of birds also thrive on the island and the surrounding areas,

Mu Ko Surin National Park.

including Beach Thick-Knee, Great-billed Heron and Large Green-pigeon. Green Imperial Pigeon, Pied Imperial Pigeon and Nicobar Pigeon can also be found on the main island.

Krabi Estuary
08°04'27.3"N 98°55'01.6"E
The estuary offers a good chance to see both mangrove species and waders. The boardwalk trail that leads to Khao Khanap Nam cliffs is a good area to look for the range-restricted Brown-winged Kingfisher, Ruddy Kingfisher and Mangrove Pitta. Alternatively, tourist boats are also available for birdwatching at the pier. Mudflats and sandspits near the delta are an important wintering area for globally threatened species such as Nordmann's Greenshank and Chinese Egret, as well as many other species of waders.

Krabi Estuary.

Ton Nga Chang Waterfall
06°56'54.7"N 100°14'08.4"E
The waterfall is located in the Ton Nga Chang Wildlife Sanctuary and is easily accessed from Hat Yai. Early morning along the road that leads to the waterfall and around the parking area is usually

productive. Scaly-breasted Bulbul, Hairy-backed Bulbul, Blue-crowned Hanging-parrot, Green Broadbill, Black-and-yellow Broadbill and Red-throated Barbet are some of the species that are frequently seen.

San Kala Khiri National Park
06°19'34.9"N 100°55'22.6"E
This park is located near the Thai/Malay border between Songkhla and Yala provinces. Many rare species of lowland forest birds have been recorded, including Large Green Pigeon, Dusky Eagle-Owl, Black Hornbill and Black Magpie. It is also one of the best places to see the globally threatened Plain-pouched Hornbill between June and October.

San Kala Khiri National Park.

Khao Nam Khang National Park
06°35'59.3"N 100°35'20.7"E
The park is easily accessible, with productive birding possible around the park's headquarters if you are unable to venture further into the park. Many southern species such as Red-throated Barbet, Green Broadbill, Black-and-yellow Broadbill, Greater Green Leafbird, Scarlet-breasted Flowerpecker and Scaly-breasted Bulbul are frequently seen here. Scarcer species, such as Rufous-collared

Khao Nam Khang National Park.

Kingfisher, Malaysian Blue-banded Kingfisher and Spotted Fantail, can also be found.

Hala-Bala Wildlife Sanctuary
05°48'26.4"N 101°50'44.4"E
Located at the southernmost tip of the country, the sanctuary is home to many species that do not occur anywhere else in Thailand. The area is also one of the few well-protected tracts of lowland forest in southern Thailand. It is best known for the diversity of hornbills, with the most iconic species being Rhinoceros Hornbill, Wrinkled Hornbill and Helmeted Hornbill. Other specialties include Little Green Pigeon, Red-naped Trogon, Malaysian Rail-Babbler and Reddish Scops Owl.

Hala-Bala Wildlife Sanctuary.

SPECIES ACCOUNTS

Lesser Whistling-duck *Dendrocygna javanica* 38–42cm

The most abundant and widespread duck in Thailand. Overall rich chestnut-brown with darker back and crown, and white undertail-coverts. In flight shows dark maroon-chestnut upperwing-coverts and completely dark flight feathers. Noisy and gregarious. Gives loud piercing whistles, especially when in flocks.

Where to see A common resident duck that can be found in nearly all kinds of wetlands. Typically encountered at freshwater sites but can sometimes be found in salt pans as well. Usually seen in large noisy flocks during non-breeding season.

Cotton Pygmy-goose *Nettapus coromandelianus* 30–38cm

A small duck with a very short, compact bill. Male is distinctive with overall white plumage and black stripes on the crown and breast. In flight shows glossy green upperwing-coverts with bold white stripes on the wings. Female is much duller, with pale greyish-brown plumage overall.

Where to see A fairly common resident in large bodies of fresh water throughout the country. Scarce and more local in the north.

Knob-billed Duck *Sarkidiornis melanotos* 64–79cm

A large and distinctive duck with a whitish body and glossy black upperparts. Head has variable amounts of blackish spots. Male has a large knob on the bill during breeding season.

Where to see A rare winter visitor to large bodies of fresh water in the north, centre, and north-east. Locally common in the south where it breeds in wetlands and rice fields with tall Asian Palmyra Palms.

Garganey *Spatula querquedula* 37–41cm

A rather small duck with a relatively long dark bill. Male is easily distinguished by the long white eyebrow, pale grey flanks, and grey upperwing-coverts. Female and eclipse male are mottled brown overall with dark stripes on the face and crown.

Where to see A common and widespread winter visitor to large waterbodies. Scarcer and less numerous in the south. Can be found in freshwater wetlands, salt pans and aquaculture ponds.

Indian Spot-billed Duck *Anas poecilorhyncha* 58–63cm

A large duck with a distinctive black-and-yellow bill. Sexes are similar with overall pale greyish-brown plumage and a darker back. Has a short dark eye-stripe, white wing panel and glossy blue or green patch on the wings.

Where to see An uncommon or locally common resident and winter visitor in the north and north-east. Usually found in large bodies of fresh water but pairs may stray into rice fields during breeding season.

Chinese Francolin *Francolinus pintadeanus* 31–34cm

A large partridge with overall black-and-white plumage. Male has bold black stripes on the head with small black and white spots across the body. Female has barred plumage. Legs are bright yellow, with rufous undertail-coverts.

Where to see A fairly common resident of forest edge, grassland, scrub, and cultivated areas, except in the south. Extremely shy and difficult to see even though males can be very vocal during the breeding season.

Rufous-throated Partridge *Arborophila rufogularis* 26–29cm

A beautiful and intricately patterned partridge. Breast is silvery-grey with white and chestnut spots on the flanks. Upperparts are olive-brown with buffish and black wing-bars. Head has bold black and white spots and a bright orange throat patch.

Where to see An uncommon to locally common resident of evergreen forest on high mountains in the north and west. Vocal but shy. Usually seen in pairs or small flocks walking on the damp forest floor.

Bar-backed Partridge *Arborophila brunneopectus* 26–29cm

A round sandy-brown bird with striking head and body patterns. Thin black barring on the back can be quite difficult to see, despite the name. Flanks have bold white spots with black scales.

Where to see
An uncommon bird of evergreen forest and mixed-deciduous forest, except in the south and south-east. Typically seen in pairs or small family flocks.

Scaly-breasted Partridge *Tropicoperdix chloropus* 27–31cm

A round ball-like bird with overall brown plumage. Whitish face and orange neck are heavily spotted. Breast and upperparts are finely barred, with bolder black scales on the flanks. Legs are typically greenish-yellow.

Where to see A fairly common partridge of lowland forests and foothills. Typically found in evergreen and mixed-deciduous forest. More often heard than seen; mainly vocal at dawn.

Mountain Bamboo Partridge *Bambusicola fytchii* 32–37cm

A large partridge with brown but heavily marked plumage. Throat is buffier than the rest of the body, with a long white supercilium and chestnut stripes on the head and neck. Male has black eye-stripe while female has chestnut eye-stripe.

Where to see An uncommon resident bird of grassy patches, scrub and forest clearings on high mountains in the north. Usually seen in pairs or small flocks. Flushes up to perch on trees when disturbed.

Red Junglefowl *Gallus gallus* 65–78cm (male), 41–48cm (female)

The ancestor of domestic chickens. Male has brightly coloured plumage with long golden plumes on the neck and back, and a pair of long glossy central tail feathers. Population in the east has a white ear patch on the bare red facial skin. Female is smaller with overall rufous-brown plumage and a yellowish neck.

Where to see Found in various types of forests throughout the country. Typically occurs in evergreen forest but also ventures to forest edge and in plantations. Relatively common in protected areas but widely threatened by hunting elsewhere. Much shyer and more skittish than domestic chickens.

Mrs. Hume's Pheasant *Syrmaticus humiae* 90cm (male), 60cm (female)

Male is a beautiful and unique pheasant with an extremely long barred tail. Head and neck are glossy blue with a dark chestnut body and white wing patches. Female is warm brown overall with white scales on the wings and undertail.

Where to see A scarce resident of pine and oak forest on high mountains in the north. Shy and secretive but may be seen along roads in the early morning.

Siamese Fireback *Lophura diardi* 80cm (male), 60cm (female)

Thailand's national bird. Male is distinctive with overall bluish-grey plumage, long, glossy and curly tail feathers, bright red facial skin and legs, and a short bushy crest. Female is rich chestnut overall with heavily barred wings and tail.

Where to see An uncommon resident of lowland forest and foothills. Typically found in small family groups in dry evergreen forest.

Kalij Pheasant *Lophura leucomelanos* 63–74cm (male), 50–60cm (female)

Male has pale grey neck and upperparts, with glossy black underparts and a long pointed crest. Female is warm brown overall with bold white scales throughout the plumage. Population in south-west has bright red legs (grey elsewhere).

Where to see An uncommon to locally common resident of evergreen forest, mixed-deciduous forest and secondary forest in the west. Usually seen in small family groups.

Silver Pheasant *Lophura nycthemera* 67–100cm (male), 61–70cm (female)

Male is distinctive with overall silvery-white upperparts and tail, black underparts, and a short bushy crest. Female is warm brown overall with finely and indistinctly streaked underparts. Males in the south-east have greyish upperparts with bold black scales, similar to Kalij Pheasant.

Where to see
An uncommon resident of hill evergreen forest in the north, north-east and south-east. No overlap with Kalij Pheasant.

Green Peafowl *Pavo muticus* 180–250cm (male), 100–110cm (female)

Unmistakable. Both sexes have overall emerald-green plumage with more bluish wings, rufous flight feathers and a long erect crest. Male has an extremely long 'train' during breeding season.

Where to see A scarce or locally common resident of lowland deciduous forest and mixed-deciduous forest in the north and west. Introduced populations and hybrids with Indian Peafowl can be found in other regions.

Great Argus   *Argusianus argus* 160–200cm (male), 72–76cm (female)

A distinctive, very large pheasant with dark chocolate-brown plumage and a small blue head. Male has extremely long wings and tail that are used in courtship display. Gives a series of extremely loud and echoing calls that can be heard from kilometres away.

Where to see
An uncommon resident of evergreen forest in the south. Extremely shy and more usually heard than seen.

Great Eared Nightjar   *Lyncornis macrotis* 31–40cm

Unmistakably large for a nightjar. In flight shows very long and narrow wings and tail. At rest, a pair of long and erect ear-tufts are noticeable. Face is dark with a light buffish crown and white throat.

Where to see
An uncommon or locally common resident of lowland forests. Typically found in dry evergreen forest but may occur in urban areas during migration. Nocturnal but may be seen in flight immediately after sunset and before sunrise.

Indian Nightjar   *Caprimulgus asiaticus* 23–24cm

The smallest nightjar in Thailand. Very similar to Large-tailed Nightjar but has shorter tail, overall paler plumage, a distinct buff collar and pale wing-bars. In flight shows long narrow white outer tail feathers.

Where to see A fairly common resident in open habitats such as grassland, scrub and dry forest edge.

Large-tailed Nightjar   *Caprimulgus macrurus* 25–29cm

A nocturnal bird with long, narrow wings and tail. Sits still on the ground where its cryptic plumage blends well with the surroundings. Greyish-brown overall with a dark chocolate face, submoustachial stripe and wing-coverts. In flight shows pale patches on the wings and tail.

Where to see The most widespread nightjar in Thailand. Fairly common in open forests and plantations.

Blyth's Frogmouth *Batrachostomus affinis* 19–25cm

An unusual-looking nocturnal bird. Overall mottled brown plumage with a broad but very short bill. Male has greyish-brown plumage with black and white mottling. Female is plainer and more chestnut overall.

Where to see An uncommon bird of lowland evergreen forest, mixed-deciduous forest and secondary forest, except in the north-east.

Crested Treeswift *Hemiprocne coronata* 23–25cm

An unusual swift that is usually seen perched on branches and wires. Pale grey overall with a long, pointed crest and extremely long wings and tail. Male has bright orange face, while female has completely grey head. In flight shows very long narrow wings with a deeply forked tail that is usually held closed.

Where to see A fairly common resident of dry and open forests in the north, west and east. Also occurs in urban habitats in some parts of the north.

Grey-rumped Treeswift *Hemiprocne longipennis* 21–25cm

Very similar to Crested Treeswift but male has smaller and darker rufous cheek patch, shorter tail and darker upperparts with a slight green gloss. Female lacks the rufous cheek patch. In flight shows a large pale grey patch on the rump, unlike Crested Treeswift.

Where to see A common resident of evergreen forest, secondary forest and plantations in the south and south-west. Usually seen perched on wires and open treetops.

Whiskered Treeswift *Hemiprocne comata* 15–17cm

Unmistakable when perched. Easily distinguished from other treeswifts by long white eyebrow and moustachial stripe. Male has chestnut cheek patch, while female has dark bluish cheek patch.

Where to see A common resident of evergreen forest, secondary forest and forest edge in the south. Often seen perching on wires and open treetops. Always pauses for a brief moment with wings outstretched on landing.

Silver-rumped Spinetail *Rhaphidura leucopygialis* 11cm

A medium-sized swift with broad, leaf-like wings. Tail is very short with long needle-like spines at the tips. Bright silvery rump patch is conspicuous if seen from above. At close range, thin black shaft streaks on the silvery rump may be visible.

Where to see
A common resident swift of evergreen forest and forest edge in the south. Often seen in flight mixing with other swifts.

Germain's Swiftlet *Aerodramus germani* 11.5–12.5cm

A small dark swift with a rather short tail. Overall dark brownish with a narrow pale rump patch, which can be difficult to see. Tail is shallowly forked but can appear square-ended from certain angles. Best known for its white nest made of solidified saliva, which is the main ingredient in bird's nest soup.

Where to see An abundant and increasing resident throughout every major region in Thailand. Nearly always seen in flight, except at the nest. Usually seen in flocks that sometimes mix with other swifts and swallows.

Asian Palm-swift   *Cypsiurus balasiensis* 11–13cm

A small dark swift with very long and narrow wings. The tail is long and deeply forked but usually appears narrow when closed. No white or pale rump patch, unlike other swifts. Builds a cup-shaped nest specifically in palms. Often seen in flocks circling around their nesting sites.

Where to see A common swift that can be found throughout the country. Prefers open habitats such as rice fields, cultivation, parks and open forests, especially with tall palms.

House Swift   *Apus nipalensis* 14–15cm

A medium-sized swift with a conspicuous white rump patch and throat. Typically appears rather chunky and short-tailed compared to other swifts. Tail is slightly forked but may appear square-ended at certain angles. Nests in colonies in buildings or under bridges.

Where to see A common resident swift of open habitats throughout the country. Can be found both over open forest and cultivation. Usually seen in flocks or mixing with other swifts and swallows.

Raffles's Malkoha *Rhinortha chlorophaea* 30–33cm

A medium-sized bird that resembles a squirrel while foraging. Tail is very long with bold white tips. Male has bright rufous head, back, wings and underparts. Female has pale grey head and breast.

Where to see A fairly common resident in lowland evergreen forest, secondary forest and swamp forest in the south and south-west. Usually seen in pairs feeding in the dense canopy.

Chestnut-breasted Malkoha *Phaenicophaeus curvirostris* 42–50cm

A large and distinctive bird with a very long tail and heavy ivory bill. Underparts and undertail are deep chestnut with a greyish head and glossy green wings and tail. Male has a pale blue iris while female has a yellow iris. Both sexes have red facial skin around the eyes.

Where to see A fairly common resident bird of lowland forest and foothills in the south and south-west. Typically rather shy and rarely perches in the open.

Green-billed Malkoha *Phaenicophaeus tristis* 50–60cm

A large bird with an extremely long tail. Head, neck and underparts are medium grey with darker upperparts and glossy green sheen on the wings and tail. Each tail feather has a broad white tip that can be seen from below. Bill is ivory-green with a slightly decurved tip.

Where to see The most common and widespread malkoha in Thailand. Found in various wooded habitats from urban parks to hill evergreen forest. Rather shy. Typically seen in flight with its eye-catchingly long tail.

Chestnut-winged Cuckoo *Clamator coromandus* 38–46cm

Unmistakable. A large and slender cuckoo with a long and narrow tail. Crest is long and spiky. Glossy black head and upperparts with contrasting chestnut wings, rufous throat and whitish underparts.

Where to see An uncommon breeding visitor and passage migrant throughout the country. Shy and skittish. Usually seen while visiting trees infested by swarms of caterpillars.

Square-tailed Drongo-cuckoo *Surniculus lugubris* 24–25cm

As its name implies, an unusual bird that looks like a cross between a drongo and a cuckoo. Adult is glossy black overall with a square-ended or slightly forked tail. Juvenile has white spots throughout the plumage. Bill is short, thin and slightly downcurved, unlike any drongo.

Where to see A fairly common resident and non-breeding visitor to wooded habitats. Typically seen in evergreen forest, deciduous forest and old plantations, but also occurs in urban parks during migration.

Asian Emerald Cuckoo *Chrysococcyx maculatus* 17–18cm

A small and distinctive cuckoo. Male has a bright emerald head and upperparts with heavily barred underparts and an orange bill. Female has pale orange crown with heavily barred face and throat.

Where to see An uncommon resident bird of evergreen forest in the north. Scarce winter visitor elsewhere. Typically found in forested habitats but may occur in urban parks during migration.

Violet Cuckoo *Chrysococcyx xanthorhynchus* 16cm

A small and slender cuckoo with distinctive plumage. Male is easily distinguished from other cuckoos by the overall dark violet plumage, heavily barred underparts and a bright orange bill. Female is dull bronze-brown above with a heavily barred face and underparts.

Where to see An uncommon resident of forested habitats across much of the country. Can be found in urban parks during migration.

Plaintive Cuckoo *Cacomantis merulinus* 18–23.5cm

A slender medium-sized cuckoo with a long narrow tail. Adult has grey head, dark greyish-brown upperparts and rufous-brown underparts. Some females have overall rufous-brown plumage with heavily black barring throughout. Extremely vocal during the breeding season. Male gives a series of ascending whistles both by day and at night.

Where to see A common bird of open habitats throughout the country. Usually seen in parks, cultivation, open and secondary forest. Like other cuckoos, female lays her eggs in the nest of other birds, particularly Common Tailorbird.

Banded Bay Cuckoo *Cacomantis sonneratii* 22–24cm

A slender, medium-sized cuckoo with long narrow tail. Heavily barred overall, with a white face and underparts contrasting against the chestnut upperparts. Very vocal during the breeding season but can be difficult to see well.

Where to see A common resident of forested habitats. More frequently heard than seen. Typically sings from the dense canopy.

Large Hawk-cuckoo *Hierococcyx sparverioides* 38–40cm

A large, hawk-like cuckoo, resembling a goshawk or sparrowhawk. Tail and upperparts are dark brown with a greyish head and heavily barred underparts. Throat and breast are whitish with bold rufous stripes and fine black streaks. Juvenile lacks any rufous on the breast and has more scaled upperparts.

Where to see An uncommon to fairly common bird of wooded habitats. Breeds in evergreen forest but occurs in urban parks and cultivation during migration.

Asian Koel *Eudynamys scolopaceus* 39–46cm

Large and long-tailed cuckoo with staring red eyes and a greenish bill. Male is all black with dark blue sheen visible in good light. Female has overall mottled brown plumage and whiter underparts. Juvenile is similar to female but darker with dull eyes. Extremely vocal, even at night. Male gives a series of loud *ko-el* calls, hence the name. Female lays eggs in the nests of other birds, especially Black-collared Starling and Large-billed Crow.

Where to see A common bird of open habitats throughout the country. Often seen in parks, plantations and cultivated areas.

Greater Coucal *Centropus sinensis* 47–52cm

Large and long-tailed bird that looks like a cross between a pheasant and a crow. Adult is glossy black overall with chestnut wings and staring red eyes. Juvenile is duller with barred wings, greyish iris and heavily mottled head and underparts.

Where to see A common and widespread resident in scrubby and urban habitats. Vocal though shy but often seen while crossing roads or sunning itself on treetops.

Lesser Coucal *Centropus bengalensis* 31–35cm

br.

non-br.

Very similar to Greater Coucal in breeding plumage. Note the different eye colour: black in Lesser Coucal and red in Greater Coucal. Non-breeding plumage distinctly different, with overall buffish brown head and underparts, and pale streaks on the upperparts.

Where to see A fairly common resident and migrant in wetlands and cultivation throughout the country. Shyer and less numerous than Greater Coucal. More often heard than seen.

Coral-billed Ground-cuckoo *Carpococcyx renauldi* 65–70cm

An unusual cuckoo that looks like a cross between a pheasant and a coucal. Pale greyish overall, with a contrasting black hood and a long glossy black tail. Bill and feet bright red with purplish-blue facial skin.

Where to see A scarce resident of lowland forest in the north and north-east. Shy and extremely difficult to see. Walks on forest floor like a pheasant.

Rock Pigeon *Columba livia* 31–34cm

A very successful introduced species. Plumage can be extremely variable. The typical variant is grey overall with two bold black stripes on the wing and a black tail-band. Variable amounts of glossy green and purple sheens on the neck. Other variants include dark sooty overall, white, chestnut, and various mixtures of white-and-grey plumage.

Where to see Nearly always seen close to humans. Very common in urban and cultivated areas, from cities and parks to rice fields. An indicator of disturbed or degraded habitat. Usually seen in large flocks where food is abundant.

Nicobar Pigeon *Caloenas nicobarica* 32–38cm

A charismatic pigeon with overall dark glossy plumage and a distinctive white tail. Head is dark greyish with long glossy green and purple plumes on the neck.

Where to see A scarce and locally common resident on offshore islands such as the Similan Islands and Surin Islands. Much scarcer in the Gulf of Thailand. Typically seen on the ground, but may fly up to perch on trees when disturbed.

Red Collared Dove *Streptopelia tranquebarica* 20.5–23cm

A medium-sized dove with a rather short and square-ended tail. Male has brick-red plumage with bluish-grey head. Female is dull greyish-brown overall. Both sexes have a narrow black band on the hindneck. In flight shows broad black and grey bands on the tail.

Where to see A common and widespread bird of dry and open habitats. Adapts well to urban settings, but usually more numerous in farmland especially after the harvest. Often seen perched on wires or walking on the ground in pairs or large flocks in non-breeding season.

Spotted Dove *Streptopelia chinensis* 27.5–30cm

This long-tailed dove is one of the commonest birds in Thailand. Overall brownish with a greyish head and pinkish-brown underparts. Look for the black nape patch with small white 'polka' dots. Tail is long compared to other common doves and has large white patches on the sides, which can be obvious in flight.

Where to see A very common resident that can be found in nearly all kinds of habitats, except dense forest. Mostly occurs in cities, towns, villages and farmland.

Zebra Dove *Geopelia striata* 20.5–21.5cm

A very small dove that is usually seen walking on the ground. Much smaller than any other dove, with a long narrow tail. Overall pale greyish-brown plumage with thin black bars throughout the body. Pale bluish-grey face and pinkish breast. Female has more restricted pink wash on the breast and more extensive black barring.

Where to see A very common resident in parks, cities and cultivated areas. Native population occurs in the south of the country but the species is now introduced widely across the region.

Asian Emerald Dove *Chalcophaps indica* 23–27cm

A fairly small and stocky dove with a short tail. Head, neck and underparts are pinkish-brown while the wings and back are bright emerald-green. Male has white forehead with grey crown, while female has nearly all-grey crown. In flight shows broad black and white bands on the rump.

Where to see Fairly common in forested habitats throughout the country. Often seen while walking on roads or open tracks in forest.

Pink-necked Green-pigeon *Treron vernans* 23.5–30cm

One of the most frequently seen green-pigeons in Thailand. Male has green wings and back with pale pinkish-grey head and neck, and a large, diffuse orange breast-band. Female is green overall without any bright colours. Both sexes have a grey tail with black tip.

Where to see A fairly common resident of open woodland, urban parks and cultivation in central and southern regions. Usually seen in flocks at fruiting trees like other green-pigeons.

Thick-billed Green-pigeon *Treron curvirostra* 24–31cm

One of the most common and widespread green-pigeons in Thailand. Differs from other green-pigeons by its a pale thick bill with a red base. Overall yellowish-green with grey crown and bright greenish skin around the eye. Male has deep maroon wing-coverts, replaced by olive-green in the female. Tail short and frequently pumped while resting and foraging.

Where to see A fairly common bird of forested habitats. Typically found in evergreen forest, deciduous forest, forest edge and sometimes even urban parks. Usually seen in flocks at fruiting trees.

Wedge-tailed Green-pigeon *Treron sphenurus* 30–33cm

found in lowland forest in
the south. Usually seen in
pairs or small flocks flying
over the forest or visiting
fruiting trees.

Grey-headed Swamphen *Porphyrio poliocephalus* 38–50cm

A rather large and distinctive waterbird. Has various shades of blue in the plumage, with a more greyish head and conspicuous white undertail-coverts. Bill, legs and frontal shield bright red.

Where to see A common resident of freshwater wetlands throughout the country. Usually seen in pairs or loose flocks. Typically more confiding than most other crakes and rails. Forages in the open or at the edge of vegetation.

Slaty-breasted Rail *Lewinia striata* 25–30cm

A medium-sized rail with a long narrow bill. Adult has grey neck and breast, chestnut crown, and heavily barred body. Juvenile is much duller overall with dull brownish head.

Where to see
An uncommon to fairly common resident of marshes, rice fields and mangroves. Shy and difficult to see well but may venture into the open at dusk and dawn.

Ruddy-breasted Crake *Zapornia fusca* 21–23cm

A small dark crake with bright red legs. Underparts are reddish-brown with dark brown upperparts. Plain wing-coverts without any white markings. Tail short and often cocked, showing the heavily barred undertail-coverts.

Where to see A fairly common resident and migrant in rice fields, marshes and wetlands with dense vegetation throughout the country. Shy and secretive. More frequently heard than seen but may venture into the open at dusk and dawn.

White-browed Crake *Poliolimnas cinereus* 15–20cm

A small crake with overall greyish-brown plumage. Upperparts are warm buffish-brown with a pale grey head and underparts. As the name suggests, it has a short but distinct white eyebrow contrasting with a small black eye-stripe.

Where to see A fairly common resident of freshwater wetlands with dense vegetation in central and north-east regions. Scarce and local in the north and south.

White-breasted Waterhen *Amaurornis phoenicurus* 28–33cm

juv.

The most common and widespread crake in the region. Adult is unmistakable, with dark sooty-black upperparts contrasting with gleaming white underparts. Very short tail with rufous-brown undertail-coverts. Greenish-yellow bill with red base. Bright yellow legs with disproportionately long toes. Vocal but usually shy, although can venture into the open at dusk and dawn.

Where to see A common resident that can be found throughout. Typically seen in freshwater wetlands and rice fields but adapts well to urban settings. Can be seen quite easily in urban parks and villages.

Eurasian Moorhen *Gallinula chloropus* 30–38cm

A chicken-like bird that can be seen swimming or walking on the ground. Adult has blackish plumage with a browner back and distinctive white undertail-coverts. Bill is short and red with a yellow tip and large frontal shield on the forehead. Juvenile is much duller with overall brownish plumage.

Where to see A fairly common resident and winter visitor in freshwater wetlands throughout the country. Usually seen in lakes, reservoirs, marshes and rice fields.

Watercock   *Gallicrex cinerea* 42–43cm (male), 36cm (female)

♂ br.

non-br.

A rather large rail with long legs and toes. The sexes look similar in non-breeding plumage, with buffish underparts and darker brown upperparts. Male in breeding plumage is blackish overall with a bright yellow bill and red frontal shield.

Where to see A fairly common and widespread bird in freshwater wetlands and rice fields. Extremely shy and wary. Male frequently gives a series of loud and hollow calls during breeding season but is still difficult to see well.

Eurasian Coot   *Fulica atra* 36–39cm

A duck-like bird that is usually seen swimming. Easily distinguished by the overall sooty-black plumage, with a whitish bill and frontal shield. When seen on land, the feet are large with broad and well-separated webs on each toe.

Where to see A common winter visitor to large bodies of fresh water in the north, north-east and central regions. Typically seen in large flocks while swimming and diving for food.

Sarus Crane *Antigone antigone* 152–156cm

A very large and distinctive waterbird with long neck and legs. Plumage is pale greyish overall with a contrasting red head and legs. In flight shows black wingtips.

Where to see Extinct in the wild but recently reintroduced in the centre of the country. It is now a local and uncommon resident bird in wetlands and rice fields in Buriram and surrounding provinces.

Little Grebe *Tachybaptus ruficollis* 25–29cm

br.

non-br.

A small duck-like bird with a short pointed bill. Overall buffish-brown in non-breeding plumage with a contrasting dark brown cap and upperparts. Breeding plumage is much darker overall with a deep chestnut face and throat. Catches prey by diving underwater.

Where to see The only resident grebe in Thailand. Typically found in large waterbodies such as lakes, reservoirs and ponds (both natural and artificial).

Black-winged Stilt *Himantopus himantopus* 35–40cm

A unique shorebird with black-and-white plumage and extremely long pink legs. White head, neck and underparts contrasting with the black wings. Non-breeding plumage has variable amounts of black on the head and hindneck. Juvenile has greyish wash on the head, browner wings and duller legs.

Where to see Common in both freshwater and saltwater wetlands throughout the country. Often seen in flocks, particularly during the non-breeding season. Very territorial and noisy when nesting.

Grey-headed Lapwing *Vanellus cinereus* 34–37cm

A rather plain lapwing but very distinctive in flight. Head and neck are grey with a large black breast-band. Bill and legs are yellow with a black bill-tip. In flight shows flashing white wings and tail, with broad black wingtips.

Where to see A fairly common and widespread winter visitor to grasslands, wetlands and cultivation. Typically found in dense flocks resting on open ground or in flight.

Red-wattled Lapwing *Vanellus indicus* 32–35cm

A large shorebird with long yellow legs. Adult has striking head pattern with large rounded white patch on the cheek contrasting with the pitch-black head and neck. Red bill base with a small red wattle connected to the eye-ring. Sandy-brown back and wings with white underparts. Extremely loud and vocal. Gives a series of loud, piercing calls especially when threatened.

Where to see Common in various kinds of open habitats throughout the country. Usually seen in rice fields, reservoirs, grassland and even lawns or open wooded areas. Often in pairs or loose flocks.

Pacific Golden-plover *Pluvialis fulva* 23–26cm

br.

non-br.

A large plover with short bill and long legs. Overall yellowish-brown with dark mottles throughout in non-breeding plumage. Breeding plumage has black face, throat and underparts with a bold white stripe from supercilium to the flanks.

Where to see A common winter visitor to freshwater wetlands and coastal areas, rice fields and grassy habitats. Often seen in flocks with other shorebirds.

Tibetan Sand Plover   *Anarhynchus atrifrons* 18–21cm

br.

non-br.

A medium-sized plover with short bill and long legs. Upperparts, crown, cheeks and breast-sides are sandy-brown while rest of plumage is whitish in non-breeding season. Breeding plumage has black mask and forehead with a broad orange breast-band. Very similar to Greater Sand Plover

Anarhynchus leschenaultii but has shorter and smaller bill.

Where to see An abundant winter visitor to coastal habitats, especially mudflats and salt pans. Very scarce in inland freshwater wetlands.

Kentish Plover   *Anarhynchus alexandrinus* 15–17.5cm

br.

non-br.

A small plover with short bill and legs. Similar to Tibetan Sand Plover in non-breeding plumage but much smaller with a bold white collar on the hindneck. Crown is rufous in breeding plumage with black band on the forehead, face and breast-sides. Leg colour varies from dark grey to pale pinkish.

Where to see A common and widespread winter visitor. Typically found in coastal habitats but also occurs at inland bodies of fresh water, especially on migration. Usually seen in flocks with other shorebirds.

Shorebirds

Malaysian Plover *Anarhynchus peronii* 14–16cm

Male is similar to Kentish Plover with pale rufous cap, black forehead patch and black collar but differs by its rather scaly upperparts. Female lacks the black forehead patch and has mottled brown collar instead.

Where to see An uncommon and local resident shorebird of undisturbed beaches. Runs with quick steps, and pauses briefly, while foraging.

Little Ringed Plover *Charadrius dubius* 14–17cm

A small plover with short legs and a very short bill. Easily identified in breeding plumage by the obvious yellow eye-ring and bold black bands across the forehead, face and breast. Much duller in non-breeding plumage with brown breast-band and head pattern. Legs typically pale yellowish but can appear pinkish or greyish.

Where to see The migratory race is common and widespread in freshwater wetlands and rice fields during winter. The resident race breeds on sandbars along rivers and reservoirs in the north, north-east and west.

Whimbrel   *Numenius phaeopus* 40–46cm

A small curlew with a rather short downcurved bill. Eye- and crown-stripes are bolder and darker than in other curlews. Legs relatively short and bluish-grey. Several races occur in the region, differing in the amounts of dark barring on the rump and underwing-coverts.

non-br.

Where to see A common winter visitor to coastal areas, especially mudflats and rocky beaches. Scarce at inland freshwater wetlands.

Eurasian Curlew   *Numenius arquata* 50–60cm

A large curlew with an extremely long downcurved bill and long legs. Mottled brown overall with an indistinct eyebrow. In flight shows clean white underwing-coverts and a large white rump patch.

Where to see A fairly common winter visitor to coasts, especially mudflats and salt pans. Very scarce winter visitor and passage migrant at inland freshwater wetlands.

Black-tailed Godwit *Limosa limosa* 36–44cm

non-br.

non-br.

A large shorebird with very long straight bill and long legs. Bill is pink with black tip. In flight shows bold black-and-white pattern on the wings. Tail white with broad black band at the tip. Head, neck and upperparts are greyish-brown in non-breeding plumage. Breeding plumage has bright orange head, neck and breast.

Where to see A common winter visitor to coastal habitats and flooded rice fields in central and southern regions. Typically found in large single-species flocks. Much scarcer in the north and north-east, where only a few individuals are reported each year.

Common Snipe *Gallinago gallinago* 25–27cm

A cryptic-looking wader with an extremely long bill. Overall buffish-brown with bold dark brownish stripes on the crown and face. Very similar to other snipes but has much whiter underwing-coverts and a white trailing edge on the wing.

Where to see A common and widespread winter visitor to freshwater wetlands, rice fields and, sometimes, mangrove forest.

Pin-tailed Snipe   *Gallinago stenura* 25–27cm

Very similar to Common Snipe but typically has a shorter bill, steeper forehead and shorter tail. In flight shows heavily barred underwing-coverts and lacks the white trailing edge. Extremely narrow, pin-like outer tail feathers only visible when the tail is spread, especially while landing, preening or sunning itself.

Where to see A common and widespread winter visitor to freshwater wetlands, rice fields and sometimes swamps and streams in the forest.

Common Sandpiper   *Actitis hypoleucos* 19–21cm

A small shorebird with rather short legs and long tail. Buffish-brown upperparts and breast-sides contrast strongly with the clean white underparts. Flies with rapid wingbeats. In flight shows long white stripes on the wings. Always bobs rear body, unlike any other shorebird.

Where to see A common winter visitor to both freshwater and saltwater wetlands throughout the country. Typically seen along rivers, canals, reservoirs and salt pans.

non-br.

Terek Sandpiper *Xenus cinereus* 22–25cm

A small shorebird with a
disproportionately long
and upcurved bill. Legs
short and bright orange.
Upperparts sandy-brown
with white underparts.
In flight shows bold
white line along the
secondaries.

Where to see A fairly
common winter visitor to
coastal habitats. Typically
found on mudflats, sandy
and rocky beaches, but
also occurs in salt pans
and mangroves while
roosting.

Ruddy Turnstone *Arenaria interpres* 21–26cm

An unmistakable
shorebird with a short
upturned bill and short
orange legs. Upperparts
are dull brownish with
bold black mottling in
non-breeding plumage.
Breeding plumage
has bright chestnut
upperparts with a
cleaner black-and-white
pattern on the head and
breast.

Where to see A fairly
common winter visitor
to coastal habitats,
especially rocky beaches
and mudflats.

Sanderling *Calidris alba* 20–21cm

A small and active shorebird with short black legs. Appears clean whitish in non-breeding plumage, with black markings on the shoulders. Breeding plumage has rusty spots on the head, breast and scapulars.

Where to see A fairly common winter visitor to coastal areas, especially sandy beaches. Usually seen in flocks running back and forth at the edge of waves while looking for food.

non-br.

Spoon-billed Sandpiper *Calidris pygmaea* 14–16cm

A very small shorebird that resembles Red-necked Stint or Broad-billed Sandpiper. Has a unique spatulate bill, although it can be quite tricky to see while feeding. Usually hides among large flocks of other shorebirds, especially Red-necked Stints.

Where to see A rare but regular winter visitor to coastal mudflats and salt pans in the Inner Gulf of Thailand. Usually seen singly or in small flocks. Globally Critically Endangered and fewer than ten individuals recorded in Thailand each winter.

Red-necked Stint *Calidris ruficollis* 13–16cm

br.

non-br.

A very small shorebird with short neck, bill and legs. Rather nondescript in non-breeding plumage with pale greyish-brown upperparts and white underparts. Head, neck and wing-coverts turn bright orange in breeding plumage. Feeds actively in flocks along with other small shorebirds.

Where to see A common winter visitor to coastal habitats especially salt pans and mudflats. Scarce passage migrant at inland freshwater wetlands and rice fields.

Curlew Sandpiper *Calidris ferruginea* 18–23cm

br.

non-br.

A medium-sized shorebird with a long and slightly downcurved bill. Rather dull in non-breeding plumage, with brownish-grey upperparts and white underparts, but overall plumage turns bright chestnut in breeding plumage. In flight shows the distinctive white rump patch, unlike similar species.

Where to see A common winter visitor to coastal habitats, particularly salt pans, mudflats and aquaculture ponds. Much scarcer at inland freshwater wetlands.

Broad-billed Sandpiper *Calidris falcinellus* 16–18cm

A fairly small shorebird with distinctive head pattern. Compared to similar species, the eye-stripe and crown-stripes are bolder and more distinct both in breeding and non-breeding plumage. Bill is long with a slightly drooping tip and round base.

Where to see
A common winter visitor to coastal habitats, particularly salt pans and mudflats. Much scarcer at inland freshwater wetlands.

non-br.

Great Knot *Calidris tenuirostris* 26–28cm

br.

non-br.

A medium-sized shorebird with a fairly long bill and short legs. Very similar to Red Knot but slightly larger with longer bill and typically darker legs. Has bold black spots on head, breast and upperparts, with chestnut markings on scapulars in breeding plumage.

Where to see An uncommon or locally common winter visitor to coastal habitats, particularly salt pans and mudflats. Typically found in large flocks while roosting.

Marsh Sandpiper *Tringa stagnatilis* 22–26cm

br.

non-br.

A medium-sized shorebird with a graceful appearance. Legs very long and yellowish. Bill extremely thin, straight and long. Overall whitish with pale greyish upperparts. In flight shows a large white rump patch.

Where to see A common winter visitor to coastal habitats, particularly salt pans and aquaculture ponds. Much scarcer at inland freshwater wetlands.

Wood Sandpiper *Tringa glareola* 19–23cm

A medium-sized shorebird with long legs and a long straight bill. Upperparts brownish with white speckles on the back and wings. Long white supercilium with a darker eye-stripe. Legs typically greenish-yellow. In flight shows a clear white rump patch.

Where to see A very common and widespread winter visitor throughout the country. Typically found in rice fields and freshwater wetlands but can also be seen in salt pans.

non-br.

Common Redshank *Tringa totanus* 27–29cm

A medium-sized shorebird with long straight bill and long legs. Upperparts are warm brownish with white underparts. In flight shows conspicuous white rump and secondaries contrasting with the black wingtips. Legs more orange than red.

Where to see A common winter visitor to coastal habitats including mudflats, salt pans and aquaculture ponds. Much scarcer at inland freshwater wetlands.

Nordmann's Greenshank *Tringa guttifer* 28.5–34cm

A globally Endangered shorebird. Overall pale greyish-brown with clean white underparts. Bill is thick, long and slightly upcurved with yellowish base and blackish tip. Legs more yellowish and shorter than in Common Greenshank.

Where to see A scarce but locally common winter visitor to coastal mudflats and salt pans. Normally roosts in large flocks with Great Knots, Grey Plovers *Pluvialis squatarola* and Bar-tailed Godwits *Limosa lapponica*.

Common Greenshank *Tringa nebularia* 30–35cm

A fairly large shorebird with long bill and legs. White throat and underparts with mottled greyish upperparts. Bill and legs are yellowish-green with black bill-tip. Often confused with Marsh Sandpiper but larger with much thicker bill. In flight shows conspicuous white rump.

Where to see A common winter visitor to coastal areas, particularly salt pans and mudflats. Much scarcer in freshwater wetlands but occurs in small numbers along large rivers, lakes and reservoirs.

non-br.

Bronze-winged Jacana *Metopidius indicus* 28–31cm

juv.

Adult is unmistakable. Head, neck and underparts are black with green and purple gloss. Has distinctive white eyebrow and bronze-brown wings. Juvenile has white face, neck and underparts, a chestnut crown and buffish wash on the breast. Legs long with extremely long toes and nails.

Where to see Fairly common resident of freshwater wetlands, particularly in central and southern regions. Often seen walking on floating vegetation.

Pheasant-tailed Jacana *Hydrophasianus chirurgus* 39–58cm

A graceful and unusual waterbird. Adult is distinctive in breeding plumage with long narrow tail and golden nape patch. Face, neck and wings are white contrasting with the dark brownish body. Much duller and lacks the long tail feathers in non-breeding plumage. In flight shows distinctive white wings with black wingtips.

Where to see A fairly common winter visitor to freshwater wetlands across most of the country. Breeds in large bodies of fresh water in the central region. Walks on floating vegetation and occasionally swims.

Oriental Pratincole *Glareola maldivarum* 23–25cm

An unusual shorebird that looks like a cross between a swallow and a wader. Overall sandy-brown with a distinctive black collar on the throat. In flight shows a large white rump patch, long and narrow wings with deep chestnut underwing-coverts.

Where to see A common and widespread breeding visitor. Typically found in dry grassland, areas of cultivation and dried-up reservoirs. Flies swiftly and catches prey in flight like swallows or swifts.

Small Pratincole *Glareola lactea* 15.5–19cm

A plain but exceptionally adorable bird. Sandy-brown overall with long and narrow black wingtips. Eyes are large and dark with a small black loral patch and red bill base. In flight shows prominent white stripes on the wings.

Where to see An uncommon to locally common resident of riverine habitats, reservoirs and any sort of open bare ground. Blends perfectly with sand and rocks while roosting.

Barred Buttonquail *Turnix suscitator* 13.5–17.5cm

A small quail-like bird with startling white eyes. Easily told from other buttonquails by the pale grey legs and rufous belly. Female is larger than the male with bold black patch on throat and breast.

Where to see A common resident in open grassland, scrub, rice fields, cultivation and open forest edge. Often found on roads or flushed from short grass.

Greater Painted-snipe *Rostratula benghalensis* 23–28cm

An unusual snipe-like bird with reversed sex roles. Female larger and more brightly coloured than the male, with chestnut head and uniformly dark wings. Male has mottled brown head and breast, with pale buffish spots across the wings and upperparts. Female takes no part in incubating the eggs or raising the chicks.

Where to see A fairly common resident of wetlands and rice fields. Typically seen in freshwater wetlands but may occur near mangroves. Crepuscular and difficult to detect during the day.

Brown-headed Gull *Chroicocephalus brunnicephalus* 41–45cm

A medium-sized gull with pale grey upperparts and black wingtips. Adult has white spots near the wingtips with black lores and ear-coverts in non-breeding plumage. Head turns blackish-brown in breeding plumage. Iris white in the adult and dark in the juvenile.

Where to see A common winter visitor to coastal areas especially around the Gulf of Thailand. Scarce and irregular passage migrant and winter visitor at inland bodies of fresh water.

Little Tern *Sternula albifrons* 22–28cm

One of the few resident terns in Thailand. Smaller than other terns, with very pale grey upperparts. Easily distinguished in breeding plumage by the bright yellow bill with a black tip, black cap with white forehead and orange legs. In non-breeding plumage the bill and legs are all dark.

Where to see A common resident of coastal habitats around the Gulf of Thailand, and a winter visitor to the Andaman coast. Nests on sandy beaches and salt pans.

Whiskered Tern *Chlidonias hybrida* 23–29cm

One of the most abundant terns in Thailand. Wings appear rather broad compared to other terns. Tail short and shallowly forked. Overall white body with pale grey upperwings in non-breeding plumage. Breeding plumage is striking with a black cap and dark sooty-grey underparts contrasting with the white cheeks.

Where to see A common winter visitor to coastal areas. Often occurs in large flocks. Frequently seen at large inland waterbodies during migration.

White-winged Tern *Chlidonias leucopterus* 23–27cm

br.

non-br.

Very similar to Whiskered Tern in non-breeding plumage but typically has a distinct black patch on ear-coverts. Easily identified in breeding plumage by all-black head and underparts, and contrasting whitish wings.

Where to see A common winter visitor to coastal and offshore habitats. Often seen in flocks with other terns. Can be seen at large inland waterbodies during migration.

Black-naped Tern *Sterna sumatrana* 33–35cm

A graceful tern with overall whitish plumage. Upperparts very slightly more greyish, with a long and distinctive black stripe on the head. Juvenile has scaly upperparts and an indistinct black stripe on the head.

Where to see An uncommon to locally common resident in offshore habitats. Nests in colonies on rocky islets such as around Ko Tao and Phi Phi Islands. Individuals may stray into coastal areas during the non-breeding season.

Common Tern   *Sterna hirundo* 32–39cm

A medium-sized tern with a long and narrow dark bill. Black nape, white forehead and a black shoulder patch in non-breeding plumage. Underparts grey in breeding plumage, with an all-black cap. One of the races has a bright red bill with black tip in breeding plumage.

Where to see A common winter visitor to coastal and offshore habitats. Often seen in large flocks with other terns and gulls. Absent at inland bodies of fresh water.

Great Crested Tern   *Thalasseus bergii* 43–53cm

A large tern with a long narrow yellow bill. Head has a black cap with white forehead in breeding plumage. Has a short bushy black crest in all plumages. Wings are medium grey contrasting with the overall white body.

Where to see A fairly common winter visitor to coastal and offshore habitats. Usually seen in small to medium-sized flocks mixed with other species of terns.

Painted Stork   *Mycteria leucocephala* 93–102cm

A very large stork with long bright yellow bill. Has bare orange face and forehead. Adult is white overall with black patches on the wing-coverts, wingtips and breast-band, with a pale pinkish wash on the tertials. Juvenile is dull greyish-brown overall with no breast-band.

Where to see An increasingly common large waterbird in central, southern and eastern regions. Rare non-breeding visitor in the north. Typically found in rice fields, reservoirs and salt pans. Usually seen in flocks with egrets and herons.

Asian Openbill   *Anastomus oscitans* 68–81cm

The most common and widespread stork in Thailand. Named for its unique bill with a wide gap between the upper and lower mandibles, specifically designed for catching and eating snails. Overall greyish with a black back, tail and wingtips. Adult in breeding season has whiter plumage. Legs long and reddish.

Where to see Common in rice fields and freshwater wetlands throughout the country. Often seen in large flocks either on the ground or soaring high in the sky. Nests in large colonies, usually with other waterbirds.

Oriental Darter *Anhinga melanogaster* 85–97cm

A large waterbird with a very long and slender neck. Adult dark overall with pale throat and silvery streaks on the wing-coverts. Juvenile has whiter head and neck. Only the head and neck are visible while swimming, when it may look superficially like a snake.

Where to see An uncommon or locally common bird of large bodies of fresh water throughout the country. Breeds locally in large colonies in central and eastern regions.

Little Cormorant *Microcarbo niger* 51–56cm

The smallest cormorant in the region. Bill short with a hooked tip. Overall black in both breeding and non-breeding plumages, but has silvery spots and streaks on ear-coverts during breeding season.

Where to see The most common and widespread cormorant. Found in nearly all kinds of wetlands. Swims and dives for food. Often seen drying itself on an exposed perch.

non-br.

Indian Cormorant *Phalacrocorax fuscicollis* 63cm

A large cormorant with long and narrow bill. Iris emerald-green at all ages. Adult has dark blackish plumage with small white ear-tufts in breeding season. Juvenile is browner with variable amounts of white on the underparts.

Where to see Fairly common in large bodies of fresh water, salt pans and mangrove forest in the central region. Much scarcer and sporadic in other regions.

Black-headed Ibis *Threskiornis melanocephalus* 65–76cm

A medium-sized waterbird with completely white plumage and long downcurved black bill. Adult has bare black head and neck, while juvenile has white feathers on the neck. Some might have grey wash near wingtips.

Where to see A scarce but increasing resident of wetlands and rice fields. More abundant and widespread in the central region, but occurs in small numbers in the north, north-east and south.

Glossy Ibis *Plegadis falcinellus* 48–66cm

br.

non-br.

A medium-sized waterbird with overall blackish plumage and a long downcurved bill. Has pale speckles on the head in non-breeding plumage. Breeding plumage is much brighter with rich chestnut feathers and glossy green and violet on the upperparts.

Where to see An uncommon to locally common bird of rice fields, marshes and reservoirs. Breeds locally in central and southern regions. Usually seen in medium to large single-species flocks.

Grey Heron *Ardea cinerea* 90–98cm

A large heron with overall grey plumage. Adult has pale grey head with a long bold black stripe. Bill is yellowish in non-breeding season but turns more reddish when breeding. Juvenile is duller with less contrasting head pattern. In flight, holds the neck in 'S' shape.

Where to see A common winter visitor to large waterbodies and rice fields throughout Thailand. Can be found in freshwater and saltwater wetlands.

Purple Heron *Ardea purpurea* 78–90cm

A large and long-necked heron with overall dark plumage. Adult has chestnut head and neck with long and narrow black stripes. Juvenile slightly paler with less contrasting head and neck. Similar to Grey Heron in shape and structure but much darker overall.

Where to see A fairly common bird in freshwater wetlands and coastal areas. Can be found in all major regions but more local in the north and south.

Great Egret *Ardea alba* 80–104cm

The largest white egret in the region with an extremely long neck. Dark legs and feet in both breeding and non-breeding plumages (upper legs can turn reddish when breeding). Long and pointed yellow bill in non-breeding plumage turns completely black when breeding.

Holds neck in an 'S' shape in flight like other egrets.

Where to see A common bird in wetlands, rice fields and coastal areas. Usually seen in flocks with other egrets and pond-herons. Nests in colonies with other waterbirds.

Intermediate Egret *Ardea intermedia* 56–72cm

Very similar to Great Egret but smaller, with a shorter neck and bill. Bright yellow bill in non-breeding plumage turns black when breeding. Legs black in all plumages. Holds the neck in an 'S' shape in flight like other egrets.

Where to see Common in freshwater wetlands and rice fields throughout the country. Often seen in flocks with other egrets and herons. Seldom seen in coastal habitats, unlike Great Egret.

Little Egret *Egretta garzetta* 55–65cm

A medium-sized egret with long and slender neck. Differs from other egrets by its combination of black bill and legs with contrasting yellow feet. Adult in breeding plumage has a pair of long white plumes on the nape and long fluffy back plumes. In flight, holds the neck in an 'S' shape like other egrets.

Where to see Common and widespread throughout the country. Can be found in nearly all kinds of wetlands, from coastal areas to rice fields and aquaculture ponds.

Eastern Cattle Egret *Bubulcus coromandus* 46–56cm

br.

non-br.

A rather small egret with short bill and legs compared to other egrets. Bright yellow bill in both breeding and non-breeding plumages. Completely white in non-breeding season. Head, neck and back turn bright orange in breeding plumage. In flight, holds the neck in an 'S' shape like other egrets.

Where to see Common in wetlands, rice fields and open grasslands throughout the country. Usually associated with cattle, hence the name. Often seen following herds of cattle looking for insects and other small animals disturbed by the animals. Also follows tractors ploughing the fields.

Pacific Reef Egret *Egretta sacra* 58–66cm

dark morph

white morph

A rather bulky egret with short thick neck and short legs. Has two completely different plumage morphs. The dark morph with completely dark bluish-grey plumage is more common than the white morph, which looks basically like other white egrets.

Where to see A common resident of coastal and offshore habitats. Usually seen along rocky beaches, piers or small islets.

Chinese Pond Heron *Ardeola bacchus* 42–52cm

Rather compact for a heron. Typically holds neck in an 'S' shape but stretches it out while hunting. Breeding and non-breeding plumages look significantly different. Basically indistinguishable from other pond herons in non-breeding plumage, with streaked brown neck, brown back and the rest of the body gleaming white. In breeding plumage, the head and neck turn rich maroon-chestnut, and the back turns dark bluish-grey.

Where to see An abundant winter visitor to all kinds of wetlands throughout the country, both fresh water and salt water. Can often be found along streams, pools and lakes in forests.

Javan Pond Heron *Ardeola speciosa* 45cm

A compact heron that looks identical to other pond herons in non-breeding plumage. In breeding plumage, has pale buffish head with chestnut lower neck and dark bluish-grey back.

Where to see A common resident in rice fields, freshwater wetlands and coastal areas in the centre and south. Scarce and irregular elsewhere.

Black Bittern   *Ixobrychus flavicollis*   54–66cm

Adult is unmistakable. Blackish plumage overall with bold white and yellow stripes on the neck. Female is slightly browner than the male. Juvenile is dark brown overall with pale scales, spots and streaks throughout the plumage.

Where to see A fairly common resident in the central region, breeding visitor in the north, and a winter visitor in the south. Found in freshwater wetlands, rice fields, lakes and ponds, even in urban parks.

♀ / juv.

Yellow Bittern   *Ixobrychus sinensis*   30–40cm

juv.

A small bittern with overall yellowish-brown plumage. In flight shows yellowish-brown wing-coverts contrasting with the black flight feathers. Adult has plain or faintly streaked head and neck. Juvenile has distinct brown streaks overall.

Where to see A common resident in freshwater wetlands and rice fields throughout the country. Secretive and usually seen in flight. Hides among tall grass and reeds but might venture into the open when not disturbed.

Cinnamon Bittern *Ixobrychus cinnamomeus* 40–41cm

A small bittern with brightly coloured plumage. Adult is bright orange-brown. Female has lightly streaked neck and mottled wing-coverts. Juvenile is much duller with heavily marked neck and upperparts. Can be confused with the rarer Von Schrenck's Bittern *Ixobrychus*

eurhythmus but note the bright orange-brown flight feathers.

Where to see A fairly common resident in freshwater wetlands and rice fields throughout the country. More frequently seen during wet season. Shy and more often seen in flight, like other bitterns.

Striated Heron *Butorides striata* 35–48cm

A small dark heron with yellowish or orange legs. Adult is dark greyish-green overall with white markings on the face, throat and neck. Juvenile is browner with bold pale streaks and spots throughout the body.

Where to see A fairly common resident in coastal areas, and a widespread winter visitor except in the north-east. Can be found in various types of wetlands, from mangrove forest and salt pans to forest streams.

Black-crowned Night-heron *Nycticorax nycticorax* 56–65cm

A medium-sized heron with rather short neck and large head. Adult is whitish-grey overall with black crown and back. Juvenile is streaked brown overall. Both adult and juvenile have staring red eyes.

Where to see Fairly common in freshwater and coastal wetlands. Active at dusk and by night. Often seen in flight while leaving the roost after sunset.

Spot-billed Pelican *Pelecanus philippensis* 127–152cm

An unmistakable waterbird. Huge with a very long straight bill and large neck pouch. Neck is slim and relatively long with a short crest on the hindcrown. Adult in breeding plumage is whiter than non-breeding plumage and juvenile.

Where to see An uncommon but increasing bird of large waterbodies in central, eastern and southern regions. Typically seen in flocks with other large waterbirds.

Osprey *Pandion haliaetus* 55–58cm; wingspan 127–174cm

A large and distinctive bird of prey. Crown and underparts white with a bold dark brown eye-stripe and brown upperparts. In flight shows long and rather narrow wings.

Where to see An uncommon winter visitor to lakes, reservoirs, rivers and coastal habitats throughout the country. Usually seen perched on dead treetops or soaring above large waterbodies.

Oriental Honey-buzzard *Pernis ptilorhynchus* 52–68cm; wingspan 115–155cm

A large bird of prey with a disproportionately small head. Plumage can be extremely variable but note the small head and small bill, unlike any other species. Adult male has dark iris, while adult female and juvenile have pale yellowish iris. In flight shows long broad wings with a relatively long tail.

Where to see Common and widespread winter visitor and passage migrant in nearly all kinds of habitats. Resident populations are scarcer and typically confined to evergreen and deciduous forests.

Crested Serpent-eagle *Spilornis cheela* 50–74cm; wingspan 109–169cm

A large and bulky bird of prey with
a large head and short neck. Adult is
brownish overall with pale spots on the
underparts and bold black bands on the
wings and tail. Juvenile has pale buffish
head and underparts. Both ages have
bright yellow cere, legs and feet. Hunts
snakes as its name implies.

Where to see A common resident and
non-breeding visitor to all kinds of
forested habitats. Migratory population
may occur in open habitats, plantations
and cultivated areas.

Black Baza *Aviceda leuphotes* 28–35cm; wingspan 64–80cm

A relatively small bird of prey with an
unmistakable plumage. Overall black
with contrasting white underparts and
a long spiky crest. Has broad black and
chestnut bands on the belly and white
blotches on the wings. In flight shows
broad and rounded wings with a distinct
grey, black and white pattern.

Where to see A fairly common and
widespread winter visitor except in the
far north-east. Resident population is
scarcer and more restricted to the west,
north-west, north-east and south-east.
Prefers open woodland but can occur in
nearly all wooded habitats.

White-bellied Sea Eagle
Haliaeetus leucogaster
75–85cm; wingspan 178–218cm

A large bird of prey with short wedge-shaped tail. Adult is unmistakable with completely white head and underparts, and grey upperwings. Juvenile is mottled brown overall with white patches on the underwings.

Where to see An uncommon resident of coastal habitats and offshore islands. Usually seen soaring high in the sky or perching on exposed treetops.

Greater Spotted Eagle   *Clanga clanga*   59–71cm; wingspan 155–180cm

A large bird of prey with overall very dark plumage. Cere and feet yellow. Juvenile has large pale spots throughout the upperparts, while adult is plain dark brownish overall.

Where to see A scarce winter visitor to wetlands and cultivation. Soars high over rice fields and marshes while looking for prey. Sometimes roosts with other birds of prey, especially Black Kite.

Brahminy Kite *Haliastur indus* 44–52cm; wingspan 110–125cm

Adult is unmistakable. White head and breast contrast strongly with the brick-red belly, wings and tail. In flight shows black wingtips. Juvenile is buffish-brown overall and can be difficult to separate from other species.

Where to see A common resident in wetlands and coastal habitats. Rare in the north. Usually seen while soaring in a buoyant and kite-like manner.

Black-winged Kite *Elanus caeruleus* 30–37cm; wingspan 77–92cm

A rather small bird of prey. Adult has snow-white underparts with pale bluish-grey upperparts. Has a large black shoulder patch and a small black stripe across the dark red iris. Juvenile has buffish wash on the breast with brownish scales on the crown. In flight shows black pointed wingtips similar to falcons.

Where to see A fairly common but declining bird of prey that can be found in various types of open habitats. Typically encountered in rice fields, cultivated areas and forest edge. Often seen while hovering in midair.

Black Kite *Milvus migrans* 44–66cm; wingspan 120–153cm

A rather large bird of prey with overall dark brownish plumage. Wings are long and broad, with a shallowly forked tail. Resident population has yellow cere and legs with darker plumage overall. Migratory population is larger with greyish cere and legs. Juvenile has more heavily streaked plumage in both populations.

Where to see The migratory population is fairly common and widespread in open habitats throughout the country. Can be found in large numbers at certain roosting sites. The resident population is rare and very local.

Crested Goshawk *Accipiter trivirgatus* 30–46cm; wingspan 54–79cm

A bulky medium-sized bird of prey with strong thick yellow legs. Adult has dark greyish-brown upperparts, greyish face and white underparts with rufous-brown streaks and bars. Juvenile is paler overall with brownish spots on the pale buffish underparts. In flight shows very broad wings and a relatively long tail.

Where to see A fairly common and widespread resident. Typically seen in wooded habitats, from evergreen forest to forest edge and plantations.

Shikra *Accipiter badius* 30–36cm; wingspan up to 68cm

A medium-sized bird of prey with broad wings and rounded wingtips. Adult has paler grey head and upperparts compared to other sparrowhawks. Underparts white with fine rufous barring on the breast and belly. Male has dark crimson iris while female has yellow iris. Juvenile has greyish-brown upperparts, with brown streaks and spots on the underparts.

Where to see One of the most common and widespread sparrowhawks in Thailand. Typically found in open forest, forest edge, plantations and farmland.

Japanese Sparrowhawk *Accipiter gularis* 23–30cm; wingspan 46–58cm

A small and compact sparrowhawk. Male has dark red iris, dark grey upperparts, and pale rufous wash and faint barring on the breast and belly. Female browner above with yellow iris, and more distinct barring on the underparts. Differentiated from Shikra and Chinese Sparrowhawk *Accipiter* *soloensis* by having a narrow but distinct yellow eye-ring.

Where to see A common and widespread winter visitor and passage migrant. Typically found in wooded habitats but also occurs in cultivated areas and urban parks during migration.

Eastern Marsh Harrier *Circus spilonotus* 47–55cm; wingspan 115–145cm

A large and bulky harrier with very variable plumage. Male typically has white underparts, dark greyish upperparts, and either a black or white-streaked head. Female is rufous-brown overall with streaked underparts. Juvenile dark brown overall with pale buffish patches on the head, breast and wing-coverts.

Where to see A fairly common winter visitor to wetlands and cultivation throughout the country. Usually seen singly or in small loose flocks flying low above the ground.

Pied Harrier *Circus melanoleucos* 43–50cm; wingspan 110–125cm

Male is a distinctive bird of prey. Head and upperparts are black, with white underparts and white patches on the wings and a grey tail. Female has brown upperparts with streaked head and underparts. Juvenile has plain dark chestnut plumage overall. Adult has yellow iris, while juvenile has dark iris.

Where to see A fairly common winter visitor to wetlands and cultivation throughout the country. More common and numerous in the north.

Rufous-winged Buzzard *Butastur liventer* 35–41cm; wingspan 84–91cm

A bulky medium-sized bird of prey. Adult has pale grey head, yellow iris, rufous-brown upperparts and white underparts. Juvenile is similar but has dark iris and more mottled head and underparts. The bright rufous wings and tail are only visible in flight.

Where to see An uncommon or locally common resident in northern Thailand. Scarce winter visitor to the south. Prefers open wooded areas, forest edge and cultivation.

Grey-faced Buzzard *Butastur indicus* 41–48cm; wingspan 101–110cm

juv.

A medium-sized bird of prey with long and pointed wings. Adult has grey face contrasting with white eyebrow and bright yellow iris. Throat is white with a long black mesial stripe. Juvenile is buffier-brown overall with more heavily streaked underparts.

Where to see A fairly common and widespread winter visitor and passage migrant to nearly all types of open habitats, especially open forest.

Barn Owl *Tyto alba* 23–29cm

A medium-sized owl with distinctive whitish plumage. Upperparts are golden-brown with grey patches and small black and white spots. Face is typically whitish with a heart-shaped border. Appears whitish overall in flight on slow and smooth wingbeats.

Where to see An uncommon to fairly common resident of urban areas and cultivation throughout the country. Usually seen perching on poles and rooftops at night.

Collared Scops Owl *Otus lettia* 23–25cm

A small owl with distinct ear-tufts. Plumage can be quite variable, from greyish to buffish-brown. Distinguished from other scops owls by having dark eyes, a thin black border around the face and a broad buffish collar on hindneck. Call a brief and hollow *buuo*.

Where to see A common and widespread resident. Typically found in parks, plantations and lowland forest. Strictly nocturnal but may be seen at daytime roost.

Asian Barred Owlet *Glaucidium cuculoides* 22–25cm

A medium-sized owl that can be found both during the day and at night. Overall rufous-brown with black barring over the head, breast and upperparts. Head is large and round with staring yellow eyes.

Where to see A common owl of open forests except in the south. Can be found even in urban parks, as well as in plantations and forest edge. Active and vocal both by day and at night. Often mobbed by small birds during the day.

Spotted Owlet *Athene brama* 19–21cm

A small owl with a large round head. Overall, more greyish than other owlets with bold white spots on the crown and upperparts. Underparts whitish with greyish-brown markings. Eyes large and bright yellow.

Where to see A fairly common resident of open forest, parks and cultivation. Scarce and local in the north and south. Frequently seen roosting in pairs or small groups during the day.

Collared Owlet *Taenioptynx brodiei* 15–17cm

A small owl with a round head and a pair of false eyes on the back of the head. Plumage similar to Asian Barred Owlet but has spotted (instead of barred) crown with sparser and more distinct brown spots on the underparts.

Where to see A fairly common resident of evergreen forest, mainly on high mountains and in foothills. Vocal and active during daytime. Often mobbed by small birds.

Brown Boobook *Ninox scutulata* 27–33cm

A medium-sized owl that often resembles a hawk. Dark rufous-brown overall with a greyer head. Underparts whitish with bold brown streaks and arrowhead markings. Eyes large and yellow, with a small white patch on the forehead.

Where to see A fairly common resident of various forest types including evergreen forest, mixed-deciduous forest and even forest edge and parks.

Buffy Fish Owl *Ketupa ketupu* 38–44cm

A large owl with overall warm brown plumage and a pair of long ear-tufts. Upperparts have bold black markings with thin black streaks on the underparts. Eyes large and bright yellow. Typically has a prominent white patch on the forehead.

Where to see
An uncommon resident of lowland forest and foothills. May also occur in parks, plantations and mangroves.

Orange-breasted Trogon *Harpactes oreskios* 25–31cm

A medium-sized trogon with bright yellow underparts. Male has olive head and breast with rufous-brown upperparts and orange wash on the lower breast. Female is much duller with greyer head and duller upperparts. Long and narrow tail has white underside with black borders.

Where to see A fairly common and widespread resident in evergreen forest and mixed-deciduous forest. Remains very still on horizontal perches. Typically seen singly or in pairs.

Red-headed Trogon   *Harpactes erythrocephalus* 31–35cm

A large and brightly coloured bird. Male has crimson head, bright red underparts and orange upperparts. Female also has red underparts but a brown head and upperparts. Both sexes have a narrow and indistinct white breast-band.

Where to see A fairly common bird of hill evergreen forest in the north, north-east, west and south-east. Scarce and very local in the south.

Eurasian Hoopoe   *Upupa epops* 19–32cm

Unmistakable. Head and underparts are rufous-brown with a large, rounded crest that is normally held folded. In flight shows distinctive black-and-white striped wings and tail, with an undulating flight pattern. Forages mainly on the ground.

Where to see A fairly common and widespread bird in open habitats except in the far south. Usually seen on lawns, open grassland and in urban parks. Typically seen singly or in pairs.

Oriental Pied Hornbill *Anthracoceros albirostris* 55–60cm

The smallest and most frequently seen hornbill in Thailand. Head, wings and tail are black with a contrasting white belly. Large bill and casque with black markings near the tip (mainly black in female). Both sexes have pale bare skin around the eye on the neck.

Where to see Much more common and adaptive than other hornbills. Can be found in different kinds of wooded habitats such as evergreen forest, mixed-deciduous forest, forest edge and even on offshore islands. Noisy and gregarious. Often first noted by its loud screeching calls.

Wreathed Hornbill *Rhyticeros undulatus* 75–85cm

A large hornbill with distinctive white tail. Male has whitish head and breast with yellow neck pouch. Female has completely dark head and underparts with a blue neck pouch. Very similar to the smaller Plain-pouched Hornbill *Rhyticeros subruficollis* but shows a dark slash on the neck pouch in both sexes.

Where to see An uncommon hornbill of well-protected forests. Typically found in evergreen forest and mixed-deciduous forest, but may venture to forest edges and plantations. Usually seen in pairs or flocks during non-breeding season.

Great Hornbill *Buceros bicornis* 95–105cm

A large and distinctive hornbill with a bright yellow bill and casque. Wings and body are black with bold white stripes on the wings. Tail white with a narrow black band. Male has dark red iris with black front and rear ends to the casque. Female has white iris with completely yellow casque. Gives a series of loud croaking calls.

Where to see A resident of well-protected forests. Typically found in evergreen forest but might venture into forest edge and secondary forest. Usually seen in pairs or small flocks in flight or visiting large fruiting trees.

Rhinoceros Hornbill *Buceros rhinoceros* 80–90cm

Unmistakable. A large blackish hornbill with bright scarlet-and-yellow casque and bill. Undertail-coverts and tail are white with a broad black tail-band. Male has dark red iris while female has whitish iris.

Where to see A rare or locally common resident of the southernmost tip of the country. Found only in well-protected evergreen forest. Usually seen singly or in pairs.

Indochinese Roller   *Coracias affinis*   30–34cm

A large bird with a bulky head and thick bill. Appears all dark when perched but flashes bright blue and purple on wings and tail in flight. When seen in good light shows purplish-brown face and breast contrasting with the sky-blue crown and belly.

Where to see A common and widespread resident that can be found in many types of habitats from urban parks and grassland to open and degraded forests. Perches on exposed treetops, poles and roadside wires.

Dollarbird   *Eurystomus orientalis*   27–32cm

juv.

A large dark roller with a distinctive red bill. Overall dark greenish with browner head and purplish wash on the throat. Adult has bright red bill, while juvenile has dark bill. In flight shows long and pointed wings with a pale crescent.

Where to see A fairly common resident and winter visitor in open forests, forest edge and plantations. Can also be found in urban parks and coastal habitats during migration.

Banded Kingfisher *Lacedo pulchella* 39–41cm

A beautiful and distinctive forest kingfisher. Male has bright blue crown, back, wings and tail, with chestnut face and forehead, and pale rufous underparts. Female has completely rufous head and upperparts. Both sexes have bold black bars on the upperparts, crown and tail.

Where to see An uncommon resident of lowland evergreen forest and mixed-deciduous forest. Unlike most kingfishers, can be found away from water. Perches very still in tall canopy and can be difficult to detect.

Common Kingfisher *Alcedo atthis* 16–18cm

A small kingfisher with turquoise-blue crown and upperparts. Underparts are rufous-brown with clean white throat. Rufous ear-coverts with a white neck stripe and blue moustachial stripe. Male and female look similar but the male has

all-black bill, while the female has red lower mandible. Juvenile is duller overall.

Where to see A common winter visitor to wetlands, lakes, rivers and coastal habitats throughout the country. A small population breeds in the far north-west.

White-throated Kingfisher   *Halcyon smyrnensis* 27–29.5cm

A medium-sized kingfisher with bright turquoise-blue wings and tail. Large brown head and brown belly with contrasting large white patch on throat and breast. Long and pointed bright red bill. In flight shows patches of turquoise-blue, black and white patches on the wings.

Where to see A common resident kingfisher of open habitats throughout the country. Usually seen in rice fields, freshwater wetlands, urban parks with ponds or canals, and even open woodland. Often perches on roadside wires, poles or any exposed site.

Black-capped Kingfisher   *Halcyon pileata* 28–31.5cm

A medium-sized kingfisher with very distinctive plumage. Bill long and bright red. Bright purplish-blue back, wings and tail with a white collar, black cap and pale rufous underparts. In flight shows different shades of blue on the wings with black wing-coverts and wingtips.

Where to see A fairly common but declining winter visitor to central Thailand. Typically found in mangrove forest, mudflats, parks and rice fields. Also occurs in forest during migration.

Kingfishers

Collared Kingfisher *Todiramphus chloris* 23–25cm

A distinctive kingfisher with a bright turquoise cap and upperparts. Underparts typically white with a large white collar on the hindneck. Female has duller and more greenish upperparts compared to the male. Some might show faint scales or peachy wash on the breast.

Where to see A common resident in coastal habitats from mudflats to mangrove forest and salt pans. Much scarcer inland but can also occur in freshwater wetlands, parks, plantations and forest edge.

Stork-billed Kingfisher *Pelargopsis capensis* 35–41cm

A large kingfisher with a strong red dagger-like bill. Underparts cinnamon-buff with contrasting blue wings and tail. Head has a dark greyish-brown cap with bright red bill. In flight shows a broad pale blue rump patch.

Where to see An uncommon to fairly common resident kingfisher except in the north-east. Usually seen along large rivers, lakes, reservoirs in or near forest, parks and plantations.

Brown-winged Kingfisher   *Pelargopsis amauroptera* 35–37cm

A large kingfisher with a strong red dagger-like bill. Resembles the closely related Stork-billed Kingfisher but has brown instead of blue wings and tail. Head and underparts bright orange-brown with no greyish-brown cap. Rump has a large pale blue patch that is usually concealed by the wings but very prominent in flight.

Where to see
An uncommon resident of mangrove forest along the south-west coast.

Pied Kingfisher   *Ceryle rudis* 25–30.5cm

Unmistakable with black-and-white plumage. Bill is long and completely black. Male has two black bands across the breast while female has a broken breast-band. Both sexes have a long and bushy crest.

Where to see An uncommon to fairly common resident except in the south. Usually seen hovering above rivers, lakes and canals. Typically seen singly or in pairs but may gather in small flocks in non-breeding season.

Blue-bearded Bee-eater *Nyctyornis athertoni* 31–35cm

A large forest bee-eater with overall green plumage. Bill long and slightly downcurved. Underparts yellowish with green streaks. Forehead and throat bright turquoise-blue. Juvenile has plainer green plumage with no blue on the head and throat.

Where to see A fairly common resident in various types of forests except in the south. Typically found in evergreen forest, deciduous forest and forest edge. Often seen singly or in pairs.

Blue-tailed Bee-eater *Merops philippinus* 28–30cm

A medium-sized bee-eater with overall green plumage and a long slightly decurved bill. Adult has olive crown, orange throat and bright blue tail with a pair of elongated central feathers. Juvenile is duller overall and lacks the elongated tail feathers.

Where to see A common bird in farmland and grassland throughout the country except in the far north-east. Can be found year-round in the central region but is strictly a breeding visitor in the north. Perches in the open and catches prey in flight.

Blue-throated Bee-eater *Merops viridis* 21–23.5cm

Adult is a beautiful bird with green wings and underparts, deep chestnut crown, and bright blue throat, rump and tail. Adult has a pair of elongated central tail feathers. In flight shows rufous-brown underwing with pointed wingtips. Juvenile has green crown with duller greenish-blue throat.

Where to see An uncommon to locally common breeding visitor in the south, west, central and eastern regions. Typically found in dry open habitats where it perches on wires and exposed branches.

Chestnut-headed Bee-eater *Merops leschenaulti* 20–22.5cm

An attractive and brightly coloured bee-eater. Adult has bright chestnut crown, yellow throat, green wings and tail, with a sky-blue rump patch. Juvenile is much duller overall with a greenish crown. Lacks elongated tail feathers at all ages.

Where to see A fairly common resident and short-distance migrant. Typically found in open forest but also occurs in cultivated areas on migration. Usually seen in pairs or medium-sized to large flocks.

Asian Green Bee-eater *Merops orientalis* 16–18cm

A slender bird with overall green plumage and a long slightly decurved bill. Adult has bright orange crown, pale blue throat, narrow black mask and a pair of elongated central tail feathers. Juvenile is greener overall with green crown, more yellowish throat and lacks the long central tail feathers.

Where to see A common and widespread resident of open habitats except in the south. Typically found in grassland, farmland and open wooded areas. Conspicuous. Usually perches on roadside wires, poles or bare branches.

Coppersmith Barbet *Psilopogon haemacephalus* 15–17cm

A small colourful barbet with bright red forehead. Green tail and upperparts with streaked underparts. Has two large yellow patches above and below the eye. Yellow throat and upper breast with a large bright red band on the breast. Gives a series of repetitive hollow calls from treetops and exposed perches.

Where to see
A common bird of open woodland including urban parks throughout the country. Usually visits fruiting trees, particularly *Ficus* species. Listen for the distinctive call and look for the small nest hole with a perfectly round entrance.

Lineated Barbet *Psilopogon lineatus* 25–30cm

A large green barbet with huge pinkish-yellow bill. Head and underparts heavily streaked brown with plain green wings and tail. Has pale yellow bare skin around the eyes. More often heard than seen. Gives a series of loud hollow *poo-tok* notes and prolonged trills.

Where to see A common bird in open woodland throughout the country. Usually found in deciduous, mixed-deciduous and secondary forest, as well as forest edge, plantation and parks.

Green-eared Barbet *Psilopogon faiostrictus* 24–27cm

A green forest barbet with streaked head and breast. Overall similar to Lineated Barbet but has dark greyish bill with green ear-coverts. The sexes are nearly identical but male has a small reddish spot on the neck-side.

Where to see Fairly common in evergreen forest, secondary forest and sometimes forest edge in west, north-east and south-east Thailand. Like other barbets, more often heard than seen and frequently visits fruiting trees.

Gold-whiskered Barbet *Psilopogon chrysopogon* 30cm

A large green barbet with a thick and long bill. Has a bold and striking yellow moustachial stripe contrasting with the pale brownish face.

Where to see A fairly common resident of evergreen forest, secondary forest and old plantations in the south. Like other barbets, more frequently heard than seen. Usually seen visiting fruiting trees or perching on treetops.

Golden-throated Barbet *Psilopogon franklinii* 20.5–23.5cm

A medium-sized barbet with overall green plumage. Face grey with bright red and yellow patches on the forehead, crown and throat. Population in north-east Thailand has bold black eyebrow without any silvery streaking.

Where to see A fairly common bird in evergreen forest on high mountains in the north, west and south. Usually quite difficult to see. Perches in high canopy and visits fruiting trees like other barbets.

Blue-throated Barbet   *Psilopogon asiaticus* 22–23cm

A medium-sized barbet with overall green plumage. Face and throat sky-blue with patches of red and black on the crown and forehead. Bill short and thick with pointed black tip.

Where to see A common bird of evergreen forest and secondary forest except in the south. More often heard than seen. Perches in treetops to sing in the morning and late afternoon.

Moustached Barbet   *Psilopogon incognitus* 22–23cm

Very similar to Blue-throated Barbet but has paler blue face and throat with less red on the crown and forehead. As its name suggests, typically shows a long black moustachial stripe and a short black eye-stripe. Note that the south-west population of the Blue-Throated Barbet also has a black moustachial stripe, and identification should be made with caution.

Where to see
Fairly common in evergreen forest and mixed-deciduous forest in the north-east, west and south-east.

Red-throated Barbet *Psilopogon mystacophanos* 23cm

A medium-sized barbet with sexually dimorphic plumage. Both sexes are bright green overall with colourful patches on the head. Male has bright red throat with yellow and red patches on the head. Female lacks the red throat and yellow forehead patch.

Where to see A common barbet in evergreen forest, secondary forest and plantations in the west and south. Like other barbets, more frequently heard than seen and typically found at fruiting trees.

Eurasian Wryneck *Jynx torquilla* 16–18cm

An unusual bird with cryptic plumage. Greyish-brown overall with sandy-brown throat and underparts. Heavily mottled overall with a broad dark line on the back and finely barred underparts.

Where to see
An uncommon to fairly common winter visitor to open habitats, especially cultivation, wetlands and scrub. Scarce and irregular in the south.

Speckled Piculet *Picumnus innominatus* 9–10.5cm

An extremely small woodpecker with olive upperparts and heavily speckled underparts, short, pointed bill and disproportionately large feet. Male has a small orange patch on the forehead.

Where to see A fairly common resident of evergreen forest and mixed-deciduous forest except in the south, centre and east. Hyperactive and frequently joins mixed-species flocks.

Greater Flameback *Chrysocolaptes guttacristatus* 30–34cm

A medium-sized woodpecker with bright golden back and flashing red rump. Very similar to Common Flameback but larger with white iris and white nape. Male has bright red crest, while female has black crest with small white spots. Underparts white with black scales.

Where to see A fairly common woodpecker of deciduous forest, evergreen forest and old plantations. Often seen in pairs or singly. Frequently joins mixed-species flocks.

Common Flameback *Dinopium javanense* 28–30cm

A medium-sized woodpecker with bright golden back and flashing red rump. Smaller than Greater Flameback with much smaller bill, dark iris and all-black nape. Underparts white with black scales. Male has bright red crest, while female has black crest with small white spots.

Where to see A fairly common bird of deciduous forest, evergreen forest, secondary forest, forest edge and plantations. Often seen in pairs or singly. Frequently joins mixed-species flocks.

Freckle-breasted Woodpecker *Dendrocopos analis* 16–18cm

A small woodpecker with overall black-and-white plumage. Wings, back and tail black with narrow white bars. Face and underparts pale buffish with black spots on the breast. Male has bright red crown, while female has completely black crown.

Where to see A fairly common woodpecker of open habitats except in the south. Typically found in dry forest edge, secondary forest, urban parks and even shrubby wetlands.

Greater Yellownape *Chrysophlegma flavinucha* 32–35cm

A fairly large woodpecker with overall olive plumage and a bright yellow crest. Male has pale yellow throat, while female has dark chestnut-brown throat. In flight shows chestnut flight feathers with dark barring.

Where to see A fairly common and widespread resident except in the south. Can be found in various types of forests from evergreen forest to deciduous and secondary forest.

Black-headed Woodpecker *Picus erythropygius* 33cm

A medium-sized woodpecker with distinctive plumage. Both sexes have bright yellow throat with a contrasting black cap, whitish underparts and olive upperparts with a large bright red rump patch. Male has a small red patch in middle of the crown.

Where to see
An uncommon woodpecker of deciduous forest in the north, west and east. Usually seen in small noisy flocks and often joins mixed-species flocks.

Lesser Yellownape *Picus chlorolophus* 25–28cm

A medium-sized woodpecker that resembles the Greater Yellownape but is slightly smaller with whitish barred underparts and a white moustachial stripe. Male has red patches on the crown and throat which the female lacks. Both sexes have a bright yellow crest that continues on the hindneck.

Where to see A fairly common resident of various types of forest including evergreen forest, mixed-deciduous forest and deciduous forest, except in the south. Often joins mixed-species flocks.

Streak-breasted Woodpecker *Picus viridanus* 30–33cm

An overall yellowish-green woodpecker with whitish underparts. Male has a bright red cap, while female has a black cap. Breast and underparts heavily scaled. In flight shows black flight feathers with narrow white bars. Extremely similar to Laced Woodpecker *Picus vittatus*, but has slightly scalier breast. Best separated by distribution.

Where to see A fairly common bird of lowland forest, mangrove and plantations in the south and south-west.

Peregrine Falcon *Falco peregrinus* 35–41cm

ssp. *calidus*

ssp. *ernesti*

A large falcon with a strong and bulky appearance. Plumage extremely variable depending on the race. Resident populations typically have dark cheeks with heavily barred greyish or rufous underparts. Migratory populations have paler grey upperparts with more white on the cheeks, and whitish and lightly barred underparts.

Where to see A fairly common resident and winter visitor to nearly all kinds of open habitats. Resident populations breed on limestone cliffs.

Eurasian Kestrel *Falco tinnunculus* 27–36cm

♂

♀

A slender falcon with long wings and tail. Male has bluish-grey head and tail with rufous upperparts, while the female has a completely rufous head, upperparts and tail. Both sexes have bold black spots throughout the plumage with a broad black band on tail tip.

Where to see A fairly common winter visitor to all kinds of open habitats. Scarcer in the south.

Black-thighed Falconet *Microhierax fringillarius* 14–17cm

A tiny falcon, about the same size as a sparrow, with large head and short tail. Upperparts are black with white breast and chestnut belly. Has a broad black eye-stripe contrasting with the white eyebrow.

Where to see A fairly common resident of lowland forest, forest edge and plantations in the south and south-west. Usually seen perching on bare branches, treetops and wires.

Collared Falconet *Microhierax caerulescens* 14–18cm

Very similar to Black-thighed Falconet. Best separated by distribution, habitat and the white collar separating the black crown patch and black upperparts. Adult has white eyebrow with rufous throat, while juvenile has rufous eyebrow with white throat.

Where to see
An uncommon resident of deciduous forest in the north, north-east and west. Usually seen perching on bare branches, treetops and wires.

Alexandrine Parakeet *Psittacula eupatria* 50–62cm

A large green parakeet with a very long tail and large red bill. Bright green overall with a dark crimson shoulder patch. Male has a thin black-and-pink collar which is lacking in the female.

Where to see A scarce or locally common resident of deciduous forest and parks in central Thailand. Rare and possibly extinct in the north and west.

Red-breasted Parakeet *Psittacula alexandri* 33–38cm

A medium-sized parakeet with pale grey head and pink breast. Male has bright orange upper mandible while female has all-black bill. Both sexes have black throat and malar stripe, with whitish iris.

Where to see A fairly common parakeet in central and eastern regions. Scarcer and more local in the north and south. Typically found in open woodland, secondary forest, deciduous forest, plantations and cultivation.

Blossom-headed Parakeet *Psittacula roseata* 30–36cm

A rather small parakeet with long blue tail. Male is easily identified by the pale pinkish head with black collar. Female has grey head similar to Grey-headed Parakeet but has a black lower mandible.

Where to see An uncommon resident of lowland deciduous forest, secondary forest, forest edge and cultivation. Usually seen in noisy and fast-flying flocks.

Vernal Hanging-parrot *Loriculus vernalis* 13–15cm

A very small parrot with small bill and short tail. Overall yellowish-green with bright red rump patch. Bill and feet orange. Adult has white iris. The sexes are similar but male has pale blue wash on the throat. Juvenile duller with dark iris.

Where to see Fairly common in protected forests and forest edge where pressure from illegal poaching is low. Typically seen in flight giving the diagnostic high-pitched call.

Green Broadbill *Calyptomena viridis* 14–17cm

An unmistakable bird with emerald-green plumage, and an extremely short bill and tail. Male has black spot on the ear-coverts with black wing-bars. Female is slightly paler with no black markings.

Where to see A fairly common resident of lowland evergreen forest and foothills in the south and south-west.

Banded Broadbill *Eurylaimus javanicus* 21.5–23cm

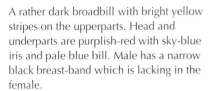

A rather dark broadbill with bright yellow stripes on the upperparts. Head and underparts are purplish-red with sky-blue iris and pale blue bill. Male has a narrow black breast-band which is lacking in the female.

Where to see A fairly common resident of evergreen forest, secondary forest and old plantations in the south and south-west. Feeds in high canopy and more frequently heard than seen.

Black-and-red Broadbill *Cymbirhynchus macrorhynchos* 21–24cm

Unmistakable. A dark broadbill with red neck and underparts. Head, wings and upperparts black with long white stripes on the wings. Tail fairly long and pointed with white stripes when seen from below. Bill is large and pale blue with yellow base.

Where to see
An uncommon resident of lowland forest in the south, west and south-east. Typically seen in pairs in evergreen forest and mangrove. Sometimes also seen in plantations and forest edge.

Black-and-yellow Broadbill *Eurylaimus ochromalus* 13.5–15cm

A small, comical-looking broadbill. Head black with a broad white collar. Breast pink, grading into pale yellow belly and undertail-coverts. Upperparts black with bold yellow stripes. Male has a complete black breast-band while female has a broken breast-band.

Where to see A common resident of evergreen forest in the south and west. Typically stays hidden in the canopy and more often heard than seen.

Long-tailed Broadbill *Psarisomus dalhousiae* 23–26cm

Unmistakable. Bright emerald-green overall with a long blue tail. Head is large with a black-and-yellow pattern that recalls a helmet. When seen from above or behind, the pale blue crown- and nape-stripes are visible.

Where to see A fairly common resident of evergreen forest and mixed-deciduous forest, except in the south where it is absent from all but the southernmost tip of the country. Usually in noisy flocks moving through tall canopy.

Silver-breasted Broadbill *Serilophus lunatus* 16–17cm

A small and comical-looking bird. Head and underparts silvery-grey with browner upperparts and rufous lower back and rump. Wings black with broad blue base to the secondaries. Black eyebrow is broad and distinctive.

Where to see A fairly common resident of evergreen forest and mixed-deciduous forest. More often seen during breeding season when its sack-shaped nest can be quite conspicuous.

Malayan Banded Pitta *Hydrornis irena* 20–23cm

A jewel-like bird that feeds primarily on the ground. Male is especially striking, with bright yellow and red eyebrows, chestnut upperparts, purple-blue underparts and reddish bars on the breast-sides. Female similar but lacks any blue on the heavily barred underparts.

Where to see An uncommon resident of lowland primary forest in the south. Shy and more often heard than seen.

Blue-winged Pitta *Pitta moluccensis* 18–20cm

A brightly coloured terrestrial bird. Bold black and buff head-stripes contrasting with the white throat. Underparts cinnamon-buff with bright red stripe in the middle of the belly and undertail-coverts. Upperparts green with bright blue wing-coverts. In flight shows large white spots on the wings.

Where to see A common and widespread breeding visitor and passage migrant. Typically found in forested habitats but also occurs in plantations and urban parks.

Western Hooded Pitta *Pitta sordida* 16–19cm

An overall green pitta with a black hood. Has a dark chestnut patch on the crown, blue shoulders, and a bright red belly and undertail-coverts. In flight shows a large white spot on each wing.

Where to see A fairly common breeding visitor and passage migrant in lowland forest. Also occurs in urban parks during migration.

Golden-bellied Gerygone *Gerygone sulphurea* 9.5–10.5cm

A tiny bird with a short black bill and legs. Greyish-brown upperparts strongly contrast with the bright lemon-yellow underparts. Face and lores usually paler than the rest of the head. Often rather vocal: male gives a series of incredibly high-pitched, musical whistles.

Where to see A common resident of coastal habitats, particularly mangroves and parks. Occasionally seen in inland plantations, as well as lowland forests.

Bar-winged Flycatcher-shrike *Hemipus picatus* 14–15cm

♂

♀

A small black-and-white bird with a long narrow tail. Male has black cap, upperparts and tail, with pale off-white underparts. Female duller and browner overall. Both sexes have a large white stripe on the wing.

Where to see A common resident of forested habitats from evergreen forest to secondary forest. Often seen in noisy flocks that forage high in the canopy. Active and frequently joins mixed-species flocks.

Large Woodshrike *Tephrodornis virgatus* 18.5–23cm

♂

♀

A medium-sized songbird with overall greyish-brown plumage. Best identified by the bold black eye-stripe and relatively large dark bill with a hooked tip. Males in the south and north-east have greyer plumage than other populations.

Where to see A common resident of evergreen forest, mixed-deciduous forest and old plantations. Usually seen in single-species flocks, but lone birds and pairs can also join mixed-species flocks.

Ashy Woodswallow *Artamus fuscus* 16–19cm

Looks like a cross between a starling and a swallow. Overall greyish with paler underparts. Pale steel-blue bill is unique among Thailand's passerines. Wings appear broad but have pointed wingtips when seen in flight.

Where to see A common roadside bird in nearly every part of the country, except the south. Usually seen perched on wires and open branches. During non-breeding season, often seen in large dense flocks.

Common Iora *Aegithina tiphia* 12.5–13.5cm

♂

♀

A small yellow bird with short bill and tail. Both sexes have bright yellow face, throat and underparts, with two bold white wing-bars. Male has darker back and variable amounts of black on the crown. Female is duller with paler wings. Male can be very vocal during breeding season, uttering a wide variety of whistles.

Where to see A common resident throughout the country. Typically found in parks, plantations, forest edge, open woodland and secondary forest.

Ioras

Green Iora *Aegithina viridissima* 11.5–12.8cm

Best identified from other ioras by overall greenish plumage with a bold yellow eye-ring. Female very similar to Common Iora but has yellowish wing-bars and a more distinct yellow eye-ring.

Where to see A fairly common resident of lowland forest and foothills in the south. Usually seen in pairs joining mixed-species flocks.

Great Iora *Aegithina lafresnayei* 13.6–15.4cm

Larger and plainer-looking than other ioras. Upperparts plain olive with bright yellow underparts. Males in the south have glossy black wings and tail, and variable amounts of black on the head. No white barring or markings on the wings. Bill long and bluish-grey.

Where to see A fairly common and widespread resident in evergreen forest and secondary forest. Typically seen singly or in pairs joining mixed-species flocks.

Ashy Minivet *Pericrocotus divaricatus* 18–21cm

A slender songbird with long narrow tail. Both sexes have white underparts and grey upperparts. Male has bold black-and-white head pattern, while female has paler grey head.

Where to see A fairly common and widespread winter visitor to open forests, parks and plantations, except in the north where it is strictly a passage migrant.

Small Minivet *Pericrocotus cinnamomeus* 16cm

As its name implies, the smallest minivet found in the region. Male has dark grey crown and back, with black face, wings and tail. Yellow underparts with bright orange breast, rump and wing patch. Female has paler grey upperparts with whitish underparts and orange rump. Females in the north and north-east have a yellow belly.

Where to see A fairly common resident in urban parks and plantations in central Thailand. Scarce elsewhere. Typically found in deciduous forest, forest edge, and mangrove forest in the south.

Scarlet Minivet *Pericrocotus speciosus* 17–22cm

Extremely brightly coloured. Male has vivid scarlet plumage with glossy black head, wings and central tail feathers. Female has bright yellow face, forehead and underparts, with grey crown and back. Has a unique wing pattern with a small and isolated bright red patch (or yellow in female) on the tertials.

Where to see A common resident in evergreen forest, deciduous forest and mature secondary forest. Often seen in flocks comprising both males and females. Typically forages in the canopy and rarely descends to lower branches.

Large Cuckooshrike *Coracina macei* 28cm

A large songbird with overall pale grey plumage. Face and wingtips slightly darker than the rest of plumage, with fine grey barring on the underparts in the female. Has a slow undulating flight and typically calls while flying.

Where to see A fairly common resident of deciduous forest, mixed-deciduous forest, pine forest and secondary forest. Population in the far south occurs only in evergreen forest on high mountains.

Black-winged Cuckooshrike *Lalage melaschistos* 19.5–24cm

A medium-sized bird with overall grey plumage. Male is plain grey with contrasting black wings and tail. Resident population in the north has darker plumage with less contrasting blackish wings. Female has finely barred underparts with broken white eye-ring.

Where to see A fairly common resident in the north and winter visitor elsewhere, except the far south. Typically found in wooded habitats from evergreen forest and deciduous forest to plantations and urban parks. Frequently joins mixed-species flocks.

Brown Shrike *Lanius cristatus* 17–20cm

ssp. *cristatus*

ssp. *lucionensis*

A medium-sized songbird with a hooked bill and long narrow tail. Conspicuous black mask contrasting with the white eyebrow and throat. Pale underparts and brown upperparts. Some subspecies have grey crown with white forehead. Female and juvenile have scaly plumage.

Where to see A common winter visitor found throughout the country. Usually seen in rice fields, grassland, wetlands and open forests; observed on exposed perches such as wires, poles and treetops.

Burmese Shrike   *Lanius collurioides* 19–21cm

Adult is a beautiful shrike with a grey crown, black mask, chestnut upperparts and whitish underparts. Female slightly duller than the male with whitish spot on the lores. Juvenile is much duller with dark scales throughout the plumage.

Where to see Breeds in deciduous and open forests in the north and west, and winters in nearly all kinds of open habitats elsewhere, except in the south.

Long-tailed Shrike   *Lanius schach* 20–25cm

ssp. *longicaudatus*

ssp. *schach*

A strikingly plumaged shrike with many subspecies in the region, all of which have white underparts with a rufous back and rump. Resident races in north and central Thailand have an all-black cap, while the resident race in the far south has a grey crown and upper mantle.

The wintering race also has grey crown but with more rufous on the back.

Where to see An uncommon and declining bird of farmland and open habitats. Usually seen singly perching on wires and other exposed sites.

Grey-backed Shrike *Lanius tephronotus* 21–23cm

Distinguished from other shrikes by its combination of clean grey crown and back, rufous flanks and rufous uppertail-coverts with dark blackish tail. Often confused with some races of Brown Shrike but has cleaner grey back and lacks the contrasting white forehead. Juvenile is much duller overall with dark scales throughout the underparts.

Where to see A fairly common winter visitor to wooded habitats. Typically found on high mountains but can also occur in lowlands especially during migration.

White-browed Shrike-babbler *Pteruthius aeralatus* 17cm

A small songbird with large head, and short bill with a distinct hooked tip. Male has white underparts with pale pinkish wash on the flanks. Head is black with long white eyebrow. Tertials bright orange contrasting with the otherwise black wings. Female is much duller with plainer grey head and greyish-olive upperparts.

Where to see A common resident of evergreen forest, and pine forest on high mountains. Typically seen in pairs while joining mixed-species flocks. Feeds in high canopy and usually more often heard than seen.

Clicking Shrike-babbler *Pteruthius intermedius* 11.5–12cm

A small and brightly coloured bird with a short hook-tipped bill. Bright yellow overall with bold black and white patches on the wings, and bold white eye-ring and grey supercilium. Male has dark chestnut forehead and throat patch.

Female slightly duller with pale rufous forehead and wing-stripes.

Where to see A fairly common resident of hill evergreen forest in the north, north-east and west. Typically joins mixed-species flocks.

Black-hooded Oriole *Oriolus xanthornus* 23–25cm

Adult is unmistakable given combination of bright golden plumage and a contrasting black hood. Juvenile duller with streaked head and breast. Bill is bright pinkish in the adult and black in the juvenile.

Where to see A fairly common resident of deciduous forest and dry evergreen forest, except in the south where it is a scarce bird of mangrove forest. Usually seen joining mixed-species flocks or visiting fruiting trees.

Black-naped Oriole *Oriolus chinensis* 23–28cm

Adult is a striking yellow bird with a long black patch through the eye. Wings and tail are black with yellow edges to the feathers. The resident population has much less yellow on the wings than the migratory race. Juvenile duller with whitish streaked underparts in the migratory race, and yellow underparts in the resident race.

Where to see Fairly common winter visitor to open woodland, parks and mangrove forest. The resident race is found only in the centre, south and south-east.

Black Drongo *Dicrurus macrocercus* 27–28.5cm

A medium-sized black bird with long forked tail. Adult has all-black plumage with bluish gloss on the upperparts. Most show a small white spot at bill base. Juvenile is similar but with variable amounts of white spotting and scaling on the underparts.

Where to see A common and widespread bird of farmland and open habitats throughout the country. Conspicuous, usually perches on roadside wires, poles or any other open sites.

Ashy Drongo *Dicrurus leucophaeus* 26–30cm

ssp. *bondi*

ssp. *leucogenis*

Similar to Black Drongo in shape and size but has paler plumage overall. Up to six different races occur, which differ by the shade of grey on the plumage and the extent (or lack) of white on the face. Resident races are large sooty-grey with no white on the face, while migratory races are much paler with distinct white around the eye and on the cheek.

Where to see Prefers more wooded habitats than Black Drongo, but can occur together in urban parks, forest edge and mangrove forest, particularly during migration. Vocal and aggressive frequently seen harrassing other birds. Often seen in acrobatic flight.

Bronzed Drongo *Dicrurus aeneus* 22–24cm

A small and agile drongo with strongly forked tail. Overall is black with bluish-green gloss on the upperparts and breast. Might be confused with Black Drongo but smaller with shorter tail and glossier plumage. Also note different habitat preferences.

Where to see Fairly common in forested habitats. Typically found in evergreen forest, secondary forest and sometimes forest edge. Absent from wetlands, rice fields and cultivation.

Hair-crested Drongo *Dicrurus hottentottus* 32cm

A large black bird with a relatively long tail and slender downcurved bill. Adult is overall glossy black with long hair-like feathers on forehead. Tail slightly forked with upward-turned outer tail feathers. Juvenile similar but duller with shorter hair-like feathers on forehead.

Where to see A common bird in open woodland except in the south. Typically found in open forest, secondary forest, and even urban parks in winter. Usually seen in flocks visiting flowering trees.

Greater Racquet-tailed Drongo *Dicrurus paradiseus* 30–65cm (depending on tail length)

A large black bird with unique tail feathers. Overall glossy black with a puffy crest on the forehead. Shallowly forked tail with a pair of extremely long outer rectrices and a spatula-shaped racquet on each tip. Can sometimes be confused with other drongos when the racquets are broken or missing.

Where to see A common resident of open wooded habitats from dry evergreen forest to urban parks. Vocal and usually mimics other birds. Often noticed while in flight, showing the distinctive tail feathers.

Malaysian Pied-fantail *Rhipidura javanica* 17.5–19.5cm

A small and active black-and-white bird. Usually feeds close to the ground and frequently fans its tail, hence the name. Overall sooty-black with white throat and underparts. Has a distinct black band across the breast and variable amount of white on the eyebrow. Vocal and restless. Gives a series of crystal-clear whistles, as well as harsh squawking calls.

Where to see A common bird in urban parks, plantations, scrub and forest edge. Less common and more local in the north, but widespread throughout central and southern regions.

Black-naped Monarch *Hypothymis azurea* 15–17.5cm

A small and active bird with relatively long tail that is often pumped. Male is unmistakable with overall azure-blue plumage, a small black patch on the hindcrown and a narrow black breast-band. Female is much duller, with greyish back, wings and tail.

Where to see A common bird of wooded habitats throughout the country. Typically found in evergreen and secondary forest, but can also be encountered in parks during winter. A regular member of mixed-species flocks.

Blyth's Paradise-flycatcher
Terpsiphone affinis
17.5–20cm (excluding central tail feathers)

♂ rufous morph

♂ white morph

♀

Male is a striking bird with an extremely long pair of central tail feathers. The typical rufous morph has bright rufous upperparts and tail with a grey head and breast. Some males have almost all-white plumage with a glossy black hood. Female is similar to the rufous male but lacks the long central tail feathers.

Where to see A fairly common resident and migrant in forested habitats throughout the country except the far north-east. May occur in urban parks or on offshore islands during migration.

Red-billed Blue-magpie *Urocissa erythroryncha* 53–64cm

Unmistakable, with black head, white belly, blue upperparts and extremely long tail. As the name indicates, bill is bright red, as are the legs. Shows strongly graduated tail with bold white tail tips on landing.

Where to see A fairly common resident in deciduous forest except in south and central Thailand. Usually seen feeding on roadkills or foraging in noisy flocks.

Common Green-magpie *Cissa chinensis* 37–39cm

A large distinctive bird with overall bright green plumage and contrasting chestnut wings. Bill and legs are bright red with a bold black eye-stripe. Some may appear more bluish, especially during the wet season.

Where to see A fairly common resident of evergreen forest and mixed-deciduous forest. Scarce and very local in the far south. Shy and difficult to see despite being vocal and loud.

Rufous Treepie *Dendrocitta vagabunda* 46–50cm

A medium-sized bird with a very long narrow tail. Head and breast are blackish, contrasting with the pale rufous underparts, rufous back, whitish wings, and grey tail with black tip.

Where to see
An uncommon resident of deciduous forest, secondary forest and dry forest edge, except in the south. Locally common at certain sites with suitable habitat. Typically seen in pairs or small flocks, as well as joining mixed-species flocks.

Racquet-tailed Treepie *Crypsirina temia* 31–33cm

A medium-sized black bird with greenish-glossed plumage. Tail is long and narrow with spatulate tip. Adult has sky-blue iris while juvenile has much duller iris. Bill is short and thick with slightly downcurved upper mandible.

Where to see Fairly common in open forest, forest edge, deciduous, secondary and mangrove forests. Usually seen in pairs or family flocks. Less common and more local in the south and north-east.

Large-billed Crow *Corvus macrorhynchos* 46–59cm

The most common and widespread crow. Overall glossy black with a thick bill. In flight shows a wedge-shaped tail. Feeds on food scraps, small animals and carcasses. Often seen in flocks, especially in urban areas and landfills. Gives a series of harsh, loud caws.

Where to see A common bird that can be found in various kinds of habitats ranging from cities, parks, cultivation to open and degraded forests.

House Crow *Corvus splendens* 40–43cm

Distinguished from the similar Large-billed Crow by having a dark grey neck and underparts instead of being completely black. Generally, appears slightly smaller as well. The native population (now extinct) had darker plumage than introduced populations.

Where to see
The introduced population is locally common in Phuket, Chonburi and surrounding areas. The native population once occurred in Phetchaburi but is now extinct.

Grey-headed Canary-flycatcher *Culicicapa ceylonensis* 12–13cm

A small flycatcher with a rather cute appearance due to the large beady eyes. Grey head with short puffy crest contrasting with the olive back and bright yellow belly. Bill is dark and tiny. Perches vertically on small horizontal branches and twigs.

Where to see Common resident in nearly all kinds of forests. Sometimes seen in urban parks during winter. Typically a leading member of mixed-species flocks.

Japanese Tit *Parus minor* 12.5–14cm

A small and active bird with distinctive head pattern. Head black with a large white patch on the cheek. Pale buffish underparts with a long black stripe on the belly, bolder in the male. Upperparts are bluish-grey with more olive-tinged back and a bold white wing-bar.

Where to see A fairly common resident of open forests on high mountains in the north. Usually seen in pairs or small flocks, and frequently joins mixed-species flocks.

Yellow-cheeked Tit *Machlolophus spilonotus* 14–15.5cm

A small unmistakable songbird. The combination of bright yellow face, long black crest and black eye-stripe is unlike any other bird. Male has a large black patch on throat and breast, while the female is duller with sooty underparts.

Where to see A fairly common resident of montane evergreen forest in the north, west and far north-east. Typically seen in pairs and frequently joins mixed-species flocks.

Sultan Tit *Melanochlora sultanea* 20–21cm

Unmistakable. An unusually large tit with black-and-yellow plumage. Male has glossy black head, wings and tail, with bright yellow crest and underparts. Female is similar but has dark olive head and breast.

Where to see A fairly common resident of evergreen forest and mixed-deciduous forest, except in the far north-east. Usually seen in noisy flocks, and frequently joins mixed-species flocks.

Indochinese Bushlark *Mirafra erythrocephala* 15cm

A small, plump, brown bird with short bill and tail. Upperparts streaked brown with whiter underparts. Has bolder black spots on the breast compared to other larks. Flight feathers are more rufous-tinged than the rest of the wing.

Where to see
A common resident in dry habitats except in the south. Usually found in open clearings near forest edge, as well as grassland and cultivated areas.

Oriental Skylark   *Alauda gulgula*   15.5–18cm

Distinguished from other larks by the small pointed bill. Overall buffish-brown with long narrow black streaks on the breast, crown and upperparts. Outer tail feathers are pale buffish. Male sings while circling high in the sky.

Where to see A fairly common resident in north, north-east, south-east, west and central Thailand. Prefers dry grassland, rice fields and cultivation.

Crested Finchbill   *Spizixos canifrons*   19–22cm

A unique bulbul with an unusually heavy bill. Yellowish-green overall with grey head and a dark tall crest. Tail has a bold black band at the tip, which is usually obvious in flight and on landing.

Where to see A fairly common resident of evergreen forest and open forest on high mountains in the north. Gregarious during winter.

Black-headed Bulbul *Microtarsus melanocephalos* 16–18cm

A relatively small bulbul with distinctive plumage. Typical morph is bright yellow overall with a glossy black hood. The much rarer grey-plumage morph has pale grey breast. Tail has bold black band near the tip, best seen in flight.

Where to see A fairly common bulbul in various types of forests except in the far north-east. Typically found in secondary forest, dry evergreen forest and forest edge. Visits fruiting and flowering trees, and often joins mixed-species flocks.

Black-crested Bulbul *Rubigula flaviventris* 18.5–19.5cm

ssp. *johnsoni*

A distinctive bulbul with overall yellowish plumage, black head and a long black crest. Population in the south-east typically has ruby-red throat. Adult has white iris, while juvenile has pale greyish iris.

Where to see A common resident in wooded habitats throughout the country. Can be found in evergreen forest to secondary forest, forest edge and sometimes plantations. Visits fruiting trees and often joins mixed-species flocks.

Red-whiskered Bulbul *Pycnonotus jocosus* 18–20.5cm

A slim bulbul with an unmistakable head pattern. Brown upperparts contrast with the white underparts and bright red undertail-coverts. Head has a long pointed black crest with a small red patch on the white cheek. In flight shows white tail tips. Juvenile is duller with yellowish undertail-coverts.

Where to see A common urban bird in the north but scarce and local elsewhere. Typically found in open woodland, parks and grassland. Native population in the south may be extinct due to poaching for illegal songbird trade.

Yellow-vented Bulbul *Pycnonotus goiavier* 19–20.5cm

One of the most common garden birds in central and southern Thailand. Overall brownish with paler underparts. Striking head pattern with dark crown and a small black mask contrasting with the gleaming white face and throat. Bright yellow undertail-coverts.

Where to see Common in urban parks, plantations, wetlands, forest edge and secondary forest. More common in the centre and south than in the north and north-east.

Sooty-headed Bulbul *Pycnonotus aurigaster* 19–21cm

ssp. *thai*

A dull greyish-brown bulbul with distinctive black cap. Upperparts greyish-brown with paler underparts. Undertail-coverts can be either red or yellow depending on the subspecies. White tail tips are usually obvious in flight and while landing.

Where to see A fairly common bulbul of dry and degraded habitats. Usually seen in secondary forest, forest edge and plantations. In central Thailand, less common in urban areas than Streak-eared Bulbul, but can be found quite easily in the north.

Streak-eared Bulbul *Pycnonotus conradi* 17.5–20cm

A medium-sized brown bird with a rather small head and longish tail. Overall olive-brown plumage with no prominent markings, except for the faint white streaking on ear-coverts. Brownish-grey iris and pale yellowish undertail-coverts. Gives harsh and noisy calls while feeding.

Where to see A common resident throughout the country. Usually seen in parks, scrubby areas, plantations and secondary forest. Often in pairs or small flocks, and joins mixed-species flocks.

Olive-winged Bulbul *Pycnonotus plumosus* 19–20.5cm

A dull brown bulbul that resembles the more common and widely distributed Streak-eared Bulbul. Also has thin whitish streaks on ear-coverts. Best identified by having dark reddish instead of greyish brown eyes and brighter olive wings contrasting with the rest of the body.

Where to see A fairly common resident of lowland forest, forest edge and plantations in the south. Usually seen in pairs or small flocks and joins mixed-species flocks.

Stripe-throated Bulbul *Pycnonotus finlaysoni* 19–20cm

A medium-sized bulbul with overall greyish-olive plumage. Adult has distinctive yellow-streaked forehead, face and throat. Underparts paler than upperparts with pale yellow undertail-coverts. Juvenile is similar but duller overall.

Where to see A fairly common bird in secondary forest, dry evergreen forest and plantations. Often seen in pairs or joins mixed-species flocks with other bulbuls.

Red-eyed Bulbul *Pycnonotus brunneus* 19cm

A medium-sized bulbul with plain brown plumage. Only differs from similar species by having orange-red iris. Juvenile (with dark iris) can be easily confused with other bulbuls and identification may not always be possible.

Where to see A common resident of forested habitats and forest edge throughout the south. Often seen in pairs or small flocks while visiting fruiting trees or joining mixed-species flocks with other bulbuls.

Spectacled Bulbul *Rubigula erythropthalmos* 16–18cm

A small bulbul with overall brown plumage. Distinguished from other similar brown bulbuls by the thin but distinct yellow eye-ring. Underparts usually appear slightly greyer than the upperparts. Juvenile is duller, with dark eyes and indistinct eye-ring.

Where to see A common resident of evergreen forest, secondary forest and forest edge in the south. Often seen joining mixed-species flocks or visiting fruiting trees.

Flavescent Bulbul   *Pycnonotus flavescens* 21.5–22cm

A medium-sized bulbul with overall olive plumage. Head is greyish with a white or buffish loral spot. Undertail-coverts are bright yellow.

Where to see A common resident bulbul of hill evergreen forest in the north, north-east and west. Usually seen in pairs or small flocks. Frequently joins mixed-species flocks and visits fruiting or flowering trees.

Puff-throated Bulbul   *Alophoixus pallidus* 22–25cm

A large brown bulbul with a tall bushy crest. Overall olive-brown with paler and more yellowish underparts. Like other *Alophoixus* bulbuls, has snowy-white puffy throat. Typically gives harsh loud calls, especially when alarmed.

Where to see A fairly common bulbul of evergreen forest and lower foothills in the north and north-east. Usually seen in pairs or small flocks while visiting fruiting trees or joining mixed-species flocks.

Ochraceous Bulbul *Alophoixus ochraceus* 19–22cm

A large brown bulbul with tall bushy crest. Very similar to Puff-throated Bulbul but note their different ranges. Overall more rufous-brown with less yellowish underparts compared to Puff-throated Bulbul.

Where to see A fairly common bulbul of evergreen forest and lower foothills in the west, south-east and south of the country. Usually seen in pairs or small flocks while visiting fruiting trees or joining mixed-species flocks.

White-throated Bulbul *Alophoixus flaveolus* 21.5–22cm

A large brightly coloured bulbul. Easily identified from other species in the same genus by the bright yellow underparts, white face and throat, with long pale yellowish crest.

Where to see An uncommon to fairly common resident of evergreen forest and mixed-deciduous forest on the western border. Typically, shy and more skittish than other bulbuls.

Grey-eyed Bulbul *Iole propinqua* 17–19cm

A small bulbul with overall olive-brown plumage. Underparts are paler and more yellowish with rufous-tinged undertail-coverts. Has a short puffy crest and greyish iris. Gives nasal, cat-like calls that can be frequently heard in suitable habitats.

Where to see A common bulbul of dry evergreen forest, hill evergreen forest and mixed-deciduous forest in the north and east. Usually seen in pairs or small flocks visiting fruiting trees or joining mixed-species flocks.

Olive Bulbul *Iole viridescens* 17–19cm

A small bulbul with overall olive-brown plumage. Nearly identical to Grey-eyed Bulbul but slightly more yellowish overall with a slightly more reddish iris. Best separated by distribution. Calls are slightly different but may be difficult to differentiate without prior experience.

Where to see A common bulbul of dry evergreen forest, hill evergreen forest and mixed-deciduous forest in the west and south-west. No known overlap with Grey-eyed Bulbul.

Buff-vented Bulbul *Iole crypta* 19–21cm

A medium-sized brown bulbul that looks nearly identical to other species in the same genus especially Olive Bulbul *Iole viridescens*. Best identified by call and distribution. Compared to Olive Bulbul, has slightly longer bill with no rufous on the undertail-coverts.

Where to see A common resident of evergreen forest and secondary forest in the south. Vocal and usually joins mixed-species flocks.

Mountain Bulbul *Ixos mcclellandii* 21–24cm

A large bulbul with a tall spiky crest. Olive upperparts contrast with the paler underparts; also has brownish head and breast. Population in the south has much greyer head and underparts. Noisy and gregarious. Gives loud piercing chirps.

Where to see Fairly common in evergreen forest on high mountains in the north, north-east, west and south. Visits fruiting and flowering trees, and frequently joins mixed-species flocks.

Ashy Bulbul *Hemixos flavala* 20–21cm

A medium-sized bulbul with large bushy black crest. Overall greyish with whitish underparts. Head is black with brown ear-coverts. Has a broad olive patch on the wing. Tail is relatively long with square-ended tip. Bill is long and narrow with pointed tip.

Where to see A fairly common resident of evergreen forest on high mountains and foothills except in the south. Noisy and gregarious. Frequently joins mixed-species flocks and visits fruiting and flowering trees.

White-headed Bulbul *Hypsipetes thompsoni* 20cm

A unique and beautiful bulbul. Overall pale greyish plumage with a striking white head. The bright red bill is short and slightly downcurved. Legs and feet are red, with rufous undertail-coverts.

Where to see An uncommon resident of evergreen forest on high mountains in the north. Usually seen in large flocks visiting flowering or fruiting trees during the non-breeding season. Best seen visiting cherry blossoms on high mountains in early spring. Scarce and difficult to detect during the breeding season.

Barn Swallow *Hirundo rustica* 15–18cm

The most common and widespread swallow in Thailand. When perched, the long narrow wings and tail are conspicuous. In flight, also shows a deeply forked tail. Dark glossy blue upperparts contrasting with the pale underparts that vary from white to rufous. Orange throat with broken dark border.

Where to see Common and widespread throughout the country in winter. Can be seen year-round in the north and parts of central Thailand. Often seen flying over open habitats, from urban and cultivated areas to open forest edges. Builds cup-shaped nest of mud that is attached to building surfaces.

Pacific Swallow *Hirundo tahitica* 13–14cm

Overall similar to Barn Swallow but has more orange on forehead with extensive orange throat and breast but no dark broken collar. Underparts are greyish with dark scales on the undertail-coverts. Tail is short and deeply forked.

Where to see A common resident in southern and south-eastern Thailand. Typically seen in coastal habitats, wetlands, cultivation and forest edge. Perches on roadside wires and poles. Builds cup-shaped nest from mud, attached to building surfaces.

Wire-tailed Swallow *Hirundo smithii* 14–21cm

A beautiful swallow with long wire-like outer tail feathers. Both sexes have clean white underparts contrasting strongly with the glossy blue upperparts and bright chestnut cap. Some birds have a peachy wash on throat and breast. Male has longer wire-like tail feathers than the female. Juvenile is duller with greyish-brown cap.

Where to see An uncommon or locally common resident of riverine habitats and irrigation canals in the north and north-east. Nearly always seen near water.

Red-rumped Swallow *Cecropis daurica* 16–17cm

Very similar to the resident Striated Swallow *Cecropis striolata*, and identification might not always be possible. Crown, back, wings and tail are dark glossy blue contrasting with the white and lightly streaked underparts. Pale orange patches on the cheeks form a thin collar on the hindneck. Adult has a large orange rump patch, which may appear whitish in the juvenile.

Where to see A common and widespread winter visitor to nearly all kinds of open habitats. Usually seen in flocks with other swallows and swifts.

Rufous-bellied Swallow *Cecropis badia* 16–17cm

A large swallow with distinctive rich chestnut face and underparts. Upperparts and crown are dark glossy blue, with a large bright chestnut rump patch that can be obvious in flight from above.

Where to see A fairly common resident of lowland forest, forest edge and even urban areas provided there are limestone cliffs nearby. Often seen perching on roadside wires or coming down to collect nesting materials from the ground.

Pygmy Cupwing *Pnoepyga pusilla* 7.5–9cm

A tiny ball of a bird. Scaly brown plumage overall with virtually no tail. Underparts can be either whitish or buffish. Song typically comprises three very high-pitched notes.

Where to see A fairly common resident of montane evergreen forest in the north. Extremely local in the south. Can be difficult to see while creeping quietly on dark forest floor.

Slaty-bellied Tesia *Tesia olivea* 9–10cm

A tiny and very active bird with virtually no tail. Long legs attached to the rear body give it the appearance of an egg with legs. Underparts are bluish-grey with olive upperparts and bright yellow crown.

Where to see A fairly common resident of evergreen forest on high mountains in the north and west. Prefers dark and damp areas, especially along forest streams.

Yellow-bellied Warbler *Abroscopus superciliaris* 9cm

A small warbler with bright yellow underparts. Upperparts and tail are olive with pale grey head, white throat and supercilium.

Where to see
A common resident of evergreen forest and mixed-deciduous forest, both in lowlands and on high mountains. Nearly always seen in or near bamboo. Usually seen in pairs or small flocks, and frequently joins mixed-species flocks.

Mountain Tailorbird *Phyllergates cucullatus* 10–12cm

Morphologically similar to true tailorbirds but not very closely related. Olive upperparts contrast with the bright yellow underparts. Face and breast are grey with orange forehead and a dark eye-stripe.

Where to see
A common resident of hill evergreen forest in the north, west and south. Shy and extremely fast. Usually seen in mixed-species flocks.

Dusky Warbler *Phylloscopus fuscatus* 11–12cm

A small brown and rather nondescript bird. Overall warm brownish with uniform wings and paler underparts. Has a long and narrow pale eyebrow contrasting with a darker eye-stripe. Fine bill with yellowish base to the lower mandible.

Where to see
A common winter visitor to scrubby habitats throughout the country, except in south where it is quite scarce. Typically found near water including reedbeds, rice fields

and mangrove forest. Quite skulking but easily located by its diagnostic call.

Radde's Warbler *Phylloscopus schwarzi* 12.5–13.5cm

A small brown warbler with a relatively long tail. Very similar to Dusky Warbler but has thicker bill, rusty undertail-coverts and mottled ear-coverts. Skulking and more often heard than seen. Feeds in dense vegetation close to the ground.

Where to see A common and widespread winter visitor except in the south. Typically found in wooded areas but can also occur in urban parks.

Yellow-browed Warbler *Phylloscopus inornatus* 10–11cm

A very small dull green warbler. Despite its name, the eyebrow is typically whitish or pale yellowish at most. Overall olive-green upperparts and off-white underparts with distinctive white wing-bars. Bill tiny and pointed with yellowish base to the lower mandible. Tertials have white tips but they can be difficult to see in worn plumage.

Where to see A very common winter visitor that can be found in any kind of wooded habitat from coastal mangrove to hill evergreen forest, as well as urban parks. Very active and difficult to see well. Usually detected by the sweet rising call similar to that of Ornate Sunbird.

Davison's Leaf Warbler *Phylloscopus intensior* 10–11cm

A small yellowish-green warbler with bold head pattern. Yellowish supercilium contrasts strongly with the dark eye- and crown-stripes. Wings and back are olive with bold pale wing-bars. Tail is white when seen from below.

Where to see A common resident leaf warbler of montane evergreen forest in the north, north-east, west and south-east. Typically found on high mountains above 1,000m.

Arctic Warbler *Phylloscopus borealis* 12–13cm

Relatively large for a leaf warbler. Usually appears dull with a strong bill and short tail. Upperparts are dull greyish-green with indistinct wing-bar(s). Underparts are whitish with pale greyish and yellowish wash on the breast and flanks.

Where to see A common and widespread winter visitor and passage migrant. Typically found in lowland forest, plantations, mangroves and urban parks.

Eastern Crowned Warbler *Phylloscopus coronatus* 11–12cm

Shares similar appearance, distribution and habitat preferences with Arctic Warbler. Distinguished from other leaf warblers by a combination of yellow undertail-coverts, white underparts, bold median crown-stripes and indistinct wing-bar. Bill is fairly long with no black on the tip of lower mandible.

Where to see A common and widespread winter visitor and passage migrant. Typically found in lowland forest, plantations, mangroves and urban parks.

Sulphur-breasted Warbler *Phylloscopus ricketti* 10–11cm

A brightly coloured leaf warbler with all-yellow underparts. Upperparts are olive with bold and very distinct black crown-stripes. Has a thin and indistinct wing-bar.

Where to see A fairly common winter visitor except in the south. Typically found in evergreen forest, secondary forest and mixed-deciduous forest, but also occurs in urban parks during migration. Nearly always seen with mixed-species flocks consisting of other warblers and small insectivores.

Ashy-throated Warbler *Phylloscopus maculipennis* 9–10cm

A tiny leaf warbler
with distinctive
grey throat and pale
yellowish underparts.
Crown- and eye-stripes
are dark and bold.
Upperparts are olive
with a narrow lemon
rump patch that is
normally concealed by
the wings.

Where to see
An extremely local
bird in Thailand.
Known only from the
summit area of Doi
Inthanon, where it is
locally common.

Oriental Reed Warbler *Acrocephalus orientalis* 18.5–20cm

A rather large warbler with
overall brownish plumage.
Underparts whitish with faint
grey streaks on the breast and a
short white eyebrow. Bill long
and narrow. Tail relatively short
and graduated. Gives variable
harsh calls while foraging, and
a complex, harsh and metallic
song in spring.

Where to see A common and
widespread winter visitor
to wetlands and rice fields
throughout the country. Often
seen singly or in small loose
flocks. Shy and secretive but
may perch in the open in early
morning and late evening.

Black-browed Reed Warbler *Acrocephalus bistrigiceps* 13.5–14cm

A small brown warbler with rather short tail compared to other reed warblers. Typically shows a distinct black line above the white supercilium. Bill short and thin with yellowish base to the lower mandible.

Where to see A fairly common and widespread winter visitor to wetlands and rice fields throughout the country. Shy and secretive. Typically stays hidden in dense vegetation but might venture into the open in early morning and late evening.

Striated Grassbird *Cincloramphus palustris* 22–28cm

A large warbler with a long and spiky tail. Overall warm buffish-brown with a paler throat and underparts. Upperparts are heavily streaked, with a long whitish eyebrow.

Where to see
An uncommon to fairly common resident in wetlands, grassland, marshes and reedbeds, except in the south and far north-east. Sings from exposed perches in the morning and evening. Feeds mainly on or near the ground.

Zitting Cisticola *Cisticola juncidis* 10.5–12cm

A tiny brown bird with incredibly loud calls. Upperparts are mostly buffish-brown with bold black streaks contrasting with the plain whitish underparts. Tail is short with a bold white tip to each feather. Male gives a series of loud clicking calls during flight display.

Where to see A common resident of grassland and cultivation throughout the country. More often heard than seen. Forages on or close to the ground but often perches on grass tops in the morning and late afternoon.

Golden-headed Cisticola *Cisticola exilis* 9–11.5cm

♂ br.

non-br.

A tiny warbler-like bird. Male is easily distinguished in breeding plumage by its bright orange head and underparts. Female and non-breeding male much duller with pale buffish underparts, orange nape and heavily streaked crown.

Tail is short in breeding plumage and long in non-breeding plumage.

Where to see A common resident in grassland and rice fields except in the south. Male is vocal and conspicuous during breeding season.

Common Tailorbird *Orthotomus sutorius* 10–14cm

Very small and active bird with long pointed bill. Olive back, wings and tail, with orange forehead and greyish nape. Underparts are white with faint greyish streaks on the breast-sides. Male has long central tail feathers in breeding season. Moves very quickly in dense shrubs. Gives a series of loud piercing and repetitive notes at any time of day. Sews large leaves together to make a vertical cone-shaped nest.

Where to see A common resident in scrubby habitats throughout the country. Often seen in parks, plantations, forest edge and secondary forest. More often heard than seen.

Dark-necked Tailorbird *Orthotomus atrogularis* 11–13.5cm

Resembles Common Tailorbird but has a complete rufous cap without any grey on the nape. Male has a large black patch on throat and upper breast, which is lacking in the female. Both sexes have yellow undertail-coverts (white in Common Tailorbird).

Where to see A common bird of open woodland. Typically found in secondary and dry evergreen forest, as well as parks and plantations. Very active and difficult to see well. Usually more often heard than seen, like other tailorbirds.

Plain Prinia *Prinia inornata* 11–15cm

ssp. *blanfordi*

ssp. *harterti*

A small rather nondescript brown bird with a conspicuously long tail. Greyish-brown upperparts with paler underparts and whiter throat. Tail has black and white markings at tip of each feather, best seen from below. Population in the north is more buffish overall. Very active and vocal. Moves quickly through dense vegetation close to the ground.

Where to see A common resident of wetlands, rice fields and grassland, except in the south. Often seen singing from open perches, including wires.

Yellow-bellied Prinia *Prinia flaviventris* 12–14cm

Much more brightly coloured than other prinias. Tail is long and narrow. Adult has bright yellow underparts with contrasting white throat and breast. Upperparts and tail olive with greyish head. Some may show short white eyebrow. Juvenile is yellowish overall with olive wings and tail.

Where to see Common and widespread. Typically found in marshes, reedbeds, rice fields and cultivation. Usually prefers wetter habitats than other prinias.

Yellow-eyed Babbler   *Chrysomma sinense* 18–23cm

A unique babbler that is closely related to parrotbills. Easily distinguished by the rufous-brown upperparts contrasting with the clean white underparts, long narrow tail, bright orange legs and reddish eye-ring.

Where to see
An uncommon resident of open grassland and cultivation except in the south. Skittish but may sing from open perches in the morning and late evening.

Swinhoe's White-eye   *Zosterops simplex* 10–11.5cm

ssp. *simplex*

ssp. *williamsoni*

A very small and active bird with yellowish-green upperparts, bright yellow throat and undertail-coverts, and pale greyish belly. Has bold white eye-ring like other white-eyes. Yellow forehead slightly contrasts with the greener crown. Resident populations have a faint yellow stripe on the belly.

Where to see A common and widespread winter visitor to nearly all kinds of forested habitats in the north and north-east. Resident populations occur in coastal habitats in the south, centre and south-east.

Indian White-eye *Zosterops palpebrosus* 9.6–11cm

yellow morph

Very similar to other white-eyes but has brighter yellow upperparts. Usually shows a faint yellow stripe on the middle of the belly. Population in the west has yellow morph with completely yellow underparts.

Where to see A common resident white-eye of evergreen forest in the north, west and far north-east. Usually seen in pairs or small to medium-sized flocks. Joins mixed-species flocks and visits flowering and fruiting trees.

Striated Yuhina *Staphida castaniceps* 13–14cm

A small babbler-like bird with short, pointed crest. Overall greyish-brown with paler underparts and white throat. Ear-coverts and nape are rufous-brown with pale streaking across the head and back.

Where to see A fairly common resident of evergreen forest in the north, west and north-east. Usually seen in large noisy flocks that move quickly from tree to tree.

Puff-throated Babbler *Pellorneum ruficeps* 15–17cm

A medium-sized babbler that is typically seen on or near the ground. Tail and upperparts are olive-brown, contrasting with the whitish underparts with narrow streaks on the breast and belly. Crown is rufous-brown with a long white eyebrow. Gives distinctive three-note call that is often heard throughout the day.

Where to see Common and widespread in open forest throughout the country. Typically found in dry evergreen forest, secondary forest and forest edge. More often heard than seen as it moves slowly through the dense vegetation.

Buff-breasted Babbler *Pellorneum tickelli* 13–15cm

Very plain buffish-brown overall with slightly paler throat and belly. Legs and tail are relatively long. Probably best told from similar babblers by the lack of any distinctive feature.

Where to see
A common resident of evergreen forest, mixed-deciduous forest and secondary forest, except in the far north-east and south-east. Shy and skulking. Usually seen in pairs foraging on or near the ground.

Chestnut-capped Babbler *Timalia pileata* 15.5–17cm

A rather large and long-tailed babbler. Head pattern is distinctive, with a reddish-brown cap, small black mask, white eyebrow and face. Iris is dark reddish when seen in good light. At close range, fine shaft streaks on the breast are visible.

Where to see A fairly common resident of open grassland and cultivation except the south. Vocal but shy and very skittish. Usually seen in pairs or noisy small flocks foraging in the dense vegetation.

Pin-striped Tit-babbler *Mixornis gularis* 11–14cm

A small and active bird that is often seen in noisy flocks. Olive-brown upperparts contrast with the pale yellowish underparts. Throat and breast have fine black streaks. Short yellow eyebrow topped by the orange-rufous cap. Population in the far south has dark iris (white iris elsewhere).

Where to see Common and widespread in open woodland throughout the country. Often joins mixed-species flocks. Gives harsh calls while moving quickly through the dense vegetation.

Chestnut-winged Babbler *Cyanoderma erythropterum* 12.5–13.5cm

A small babbler that typically appears dark in the forest shade. Seen in good light, the wings and tail are bright chestnut contrasting with the dark bluish-grey head and breast. Has pale blue skin around the eye and on the neck-side.

Where to see A fairly common resident of lowland evergreen forest in the south. Vocal but shy. Usually seen in small flocks, sometimes with other babblers.

Golden Babbler *Cyanoderma chrysaeum* 10–12cm

A small brightly coloured babbler. Bright golden-yellow head and underparts with dull olive upperparts and tail. Lores are black with fine black streaks on the crown.

Where to see A common resident of hill evergreen forest and secondary forest except in the east. Fast-moving and typically joins mixed-species flocks. Also often seen in pairs foraging actively in dense vegetation. Vocal, gives a series of repeated notes similar to a phone ringing.

Grey-throated Babbler *Stachyris nigriceps* 12–15cm

A small brown babbler
with distinctive head
pattern. Plumage is
warm brown overall with
black and white streaks
on the crown. Throat
is pale grey with broad
white moustachial stripe
bordered by a thin black
line.

Where to see A common
resident of hill evergreen
forest and mixed-
deciduous forest except
in the south and south-
east. Frequently joins
mixed-species flocks.

Rufous Limestone Babbler *Gypsophila calcicola* 18–20.5cm

A medium-sized babbler
with dark olive-brown
upperparts and more
rufous underparts. Throat
is white with bold black
streaks. Has fine pale
shaft streaks on crown,
nape and back. Legs are
dark and strong, used
for climbing on rocky
surfaces.

Where to see
An endemic species of
central Thailand with
an extremely small
distribution. Found only on a handful of
limestone mountains in Saraburi,
Lopburi and Nakhon Ratchasima.

Typically forages on or near limestone
rocks. Moves in pairs or small noisy
flocks.

Large Scimitar-babbler *Erythrogenys hypoleucos* 26–28cm

A large and bulky babbler with a long downcurved bill. Easily identified from other scimitar-babblers by grey bill and distinctive head pattern. Throat and breast are white, with dark scales on breast-sides.

Where to see
An uncommon resident of mixed-deciduous forest and evergreen forest except in the south. Vocal but extremely shy. Typically seen while visiting waterholes.

Rusty-cheeked Scimitar-babbler *Erythrogenys erythrogenys* 22–26cm

A medium-sized babbler with a long tail and long downcurved bill. Upperparts are olive-brown, white throat with rufous-brown cheeks and flanks. Some individuals may show an indistinct moustachial stripe and breast streaks.

Where to see A fairly common resident of grassy areas and forest clearings on high mountains in the north. Vocal and skittish. Usually seen in pairs or small noisy flocks.

White-browed Scimitar-babbler *Pomatorhinus schisticeps* 19–23cm

A medium-sized songbird with a distinctive long, yellowish downcurved bill. Clean white eyebrow and throat contrast with the broad, black mask. Upperparts, crown and flanks are brown with variable rufous tinge on the nape and breast-sides. Vocal. Typically gives a series of hollow hooting calls.

Where to see A common and widespread babbler of evergreen forest and secondary forest. Shy and more frequently heard than seen. Forages in pairs or noisy small flocks, and frequently joins mixed-species flocks.

Rufous-winged Fulvetta *Schoeniparus castaneceps* 10–13cm

A small and extremely active fulvetta. Distinguished from other small brown birds by a combination of striking black-and-white facial pattern, dark chestnut crown and orange wing panel.

Where to see A common resident of evergreen forest on high mountains in the north. Usually seen in noisy and fast-moving flocks. Climbs along mossy branches and tree trunks like nuthatches. Frequently joins mixed-species flocks.

Yunnan Fulvetta *Alcippe fratercula* 12.5–14cm

A small and very active
brown bird. Olive-brown
overall, with paler
underparts and a grey
head. Typically shows
a distinct white eye-ring
and black supercilium.

Where to see A common
resident of montane
evergreen forest in the
north, north-east and
west. Social and noisy.
Usually seen in flocks that
move quickly through
the dense undergrowth.
Typically a dominant
species in mixed-species
flocks.

Brown-cheeked Fulvetta *Alcippe poioicephala* 15.5–16.5cm

A small brown bird with
relatively long tail. Overall
olive-brown plumage with
greyish crown. Populations
in the south and west lack
the black eyebrow that
populations in the north
and north-east possess.

Where to see A common
resident of mixed-
deciduous forest and
evergreen forest in
lowlands and foothills.
Usually seen in flocks that
move quickly through the
dense undergrowth, and
also joins mixed-species
flocks.

Black-backed Sibia   *Heterophasia melanoleuca*   18.5–20cm

A medium-sized songbird with distinctive plumage. Blackish upperparts contrast strongly with the white underparts. Tail is long and narrow with white tips. When seen in good light, the back is browner than the rest of the upperparts.

Where to see
A common resident of montane evergreen forest in the north and far west. Usually seen in flocks or joining mixed-species flocks.

Spectacled Barwing   *Actinodura ramsayi*   23.5–24.5cm

A medium-sized songbird with a large head and long tail. Olive-brown overall with buffier crown and underparts. As its name suggests, has a bold white eye-ring and black bars on the wings.

Where to see A fairly common resident of hill evergreen forest and open forest on high mountains in the north. Usually seen in pairs joining mixed-species flocks.

Silver-eared Mesia *Leiothrix argentauris* 15.5–17cm

A brightly coloured bird that is unmistakable. Overall bright yellow with greyish back, black head, silvery-white cheeks and a broad red wing patch. Male has red undertail and uppertail-coverts, yellow in the female.

Where to see A fairly common resident of hill evergreen forest except in the east. Usually seen in pairs or noisy flocks moving through dense vegetation. Vocal and often joins mixed-species flocks.

Chestnut-tailed Minla *Actinodura strigula* 16–18.5cm

A medium-sized songbird with distinctive plumage. Underparts are yellowish with olive upperparts and rufous crown. Tail is chestnut with black border and yellow tips. Unmistakable in areas where it occurs.

Where to see Occurs only around the summits of Doi Inthanon and Doi Pha Hom Pok. Can be surprisingly tame at Doi Inthanon, where it is frequently seen hopping on the ground or feeding on leftovers. Active and vocal. Usually seen in fast-moving flocks and mixed-species flocks.

White-crested Laughingthrush *Garrulax leucolophus* 26–31cm

An unmistakable bird with a large white crest, black facial mask, white underparts and chestnut upperparts and undertail-coverts. Gregarious and extremely vocal. Gives a loud and ringing chorus while moving in flocks.

Where to see
A fairly common bird of deciduous forest, secondary forest and forest edge except in the south. Often seen foraging on or near the ground in medium to large flocks.

Black-throated Laughingthrush *Pterorhinus chinensis* 23–30cm

A dark laughingthrush with conspicuous white cheeks. Crown and underparts are dark grey with a black face and throat patch, and brown wings and tail. Songs are melodious and extremely variable.

Where to see A fairly common resident of evergreen forest, mixed-deciduous forest, secondary forest and scrubby habitats except in the south. Shy and rarely comes into the open.

Greater Necklaced Laughingthrush *Pterorhinus pectoralis* 26.5–34.5cm

A large laughingthrush with overall pale buffish-brown plumage. Very similar to Lesser Necklaced Laughingthrush but has dark iris and a complete black border around the whitish-streaked cheek patch.

Where to see A fairly common resident in mixed-deciduous forest and secondary forest in the north and west. Usually seen in flocks with other laughingthrushes.

Silver-eared Laughingthrush *Trochalopteron melanostigma* 25.5–28.5cm

A dark laughingthrush with bright yellow wings and tail. Overall, body is dark greyish with silvery streaks on the cheeks and dark rufous crown. Face and throat are black with variable amounts of dark chestnut on lower throat.

Where to see A fairly common to locally common resident of montane evergreen forest in the north and west. Typically seen in pairs or small flocks foraging on or near the ground.

Asian Fairy-bluebird *Irena puella* 21.2–25.8cm

A large chunky songbird. Male is unique, with black underparts contrasting against the bright shining blue upperparts. Female is bluish-green overall. Both sexes have red iris.

Where to see Fairly common resident in evergreen forest, except in places where pressure from poaching is high. Heavily threatened by the illegal songbird trade particularly in the south. Often seen visiting fruiting trees and waterholes.

Chestnut-vented Nuthatch *Sitta nagaensis* 12.5–14cm

A small and typical-looking nuthatch. Upperparts are bluish-grey, with greyish-buff underparts, a long black eye-stripe, and chestnut patches on the flanks and undertail-coverts.

Where to see A fairly common resident of montane evergreen forest and pine forest on high mountains in the north. Usually seen in pairs that join mixed-species flocks.

Giant Nuthatch   *Sitta magna*   19.5cm

The largest nuthatch in the world. Usually appears more like a small woodpecker. Upperparts are grey with paler underparts and chestnut scales on the undertail-coverts. Dark eye-stripe is much bolder than other nuthatches.

Where to see Globally Endangered. A scarce and local resident of pine and oak forest on high mountains in the north.

Velvet-fronted Nuthatch   *Sitta frontalis*   12–13.5cm

A small and distinctive nuthatch. Easily identified by the bright blue upperparts, pale pinkish-grey underparts and a thin bright red bill. Has a broad black patch on the forehead and pale whitish iris. Male has a thin black eyebrow. Like other nuthatches, climbs actively along tree trunks and large branches in any direction.

Where to see A fairly common resident of evergreen forest, deciduous forest and secondary forest. Typically seen in pairs or noisy small flocks. Often joins mixed-species flocks.

Hume's Treecreeper *Certhia manipurensis* 14cm

An unmistakable bird with cryptic plumage. Climbs quickly on tree trunks like a mouse. Warm rusty-brown overall with greyer underparts. Tail is long and narrow, used for supporting the body while climbing.

Where to see A scarce and local resident of evergreen forest on high mountains in the north. Active and vocal. Frequently joins mixed-species flocks.

Common Hill Myna *Gracula religiosa* 27–31cm

A robust-bodied dark myna with a large brightly coloured bill. Overall glossy black with large white wing-spots typically visible in flight. Bill is bright orange with yellow tip. Has distinctive yellow bare skin on the nape and ear-coverts.

Where to see Fairly common in protected forests and forest edge where pressure from illegal poaching is low. Also occurs on offshore islands. Usually seen in pairs or small flocks visiting fruiting trees.

Siamese Pied Starling *Gracupica floweri* 22–25cm

A medium-sized starling with striking black-and-white plumage. Bright orange bill and facial skin around eye. Distinctive white cheeks surrounded by glossy black throat, breast and nape. Typically forages on the ground in small flocks, sometimes with other mynas and starlings.

Where to see A common bird of farmland and urban parks. Less common and more local in southern and north-eastern Thailand.

Black-collared Starling *Gracupica nigricollis* 27–30.5cm

A large black-and-white starling with a striking white head and large black collar. Black bill and legs, with large yellow facial skin patch around the eye. Black wings and tail with white markings. Can resemble Siamese Pied Starling but is much larger, and has completely white head and black bill.

Where to see A common bird in farmland and urban parks except in the far south. Usually seen in pairs or small flocks. Very vocal. Gives a series of complex metallic and melodious notes.

Chestnut-tailed Starling *Sturnia malabarica* 18.5–20.5cm

A small and slender starling
with a pointed bill and
short tail. Brownish-grey
overall with paler head and
underparts. Bill is yellow
with a blue base. Outer
tail feathers are chestnut,
with pale chestnut wash on
the flanks. Some migratory
populations have chestnut
underparts.

Where to see
An increasingly common
bird of open habitats.
Typically found in open and
degraded forests, cultivation
and urban parks. Often seen
in big flocks during winter.

Vinous-breasted Starling *Acridotheres leucocephalus* 22–25.5cm

A beautiful myna with
whitish head and pale
pinkish underparts.
Upperparts are dark grey
with a large pale rump
patch. Bill and legs are
yellow with a small dark
patch of facial skin.
Typically has white iris but
some may have darker eye.

Where to see Less common
and more local than other
mynas. Typically found in
open habitats including
cultivation, forest edge
and urban parks in central,
western, south-eastern and
far southern Thailand.

Common Myna   *Acridotheres tristis* 25–27cm

A chunky myna with overall brown plumage and contrasting black hood. Bright yellow bill, legs and facial skin around the eyes. In flight, large white wing patches and white underwing-coverts are conspicuous. White undertail-coverts with bold white tail tip.

Where to see A very common bird in farmland and urban areas throughout the country. Usually seen close to humans, feeding on food scraps and nesting in building cavities and under roofs.

Great Myna   *Acridotheres grandis* 24.5–27.5cm

A large and dark myna with a long spiky crest. Overall sooty-black plumage with contrasting white undertail-coverts, wing patches and tail tip. Bright yellow bill and legs. Usually seen walking on the ground in flocks, often mixing with other mynas.

Where to see Very common in farmland and urban areas throughout the country. Can be found in the same habitat as Common Myna. Usually follows cattle or other livestock. Social and even more confident than other mynas.

Asian Glossy Starling *Aplonis panayensis* 19–21.5cm

A medium-sized starling with staring red eyes. Adult is blackish overall with greenish gloss that can be visible in good light. Juvenile has dark brownish upperparts, white underparts, with bold black streaks on throat, breast and belly.

Where to see A common resident of open habitats in the south and south-east. Usually seen in noisy flocks in urban areas, parks, plantations and forest edge. Nests in natural cavities as well as in cracks in buildings and other human-made structures.

Orange-headed Thrush *Geokichla citrina* 20–23cm

Unmistakable. A small thrush with bright orange head and underparts, and bluish-grey back, wings and tail. Some races have white shoulder patch and dark bars on the face.

Where to see A fairly common and widespread resident and winter visitor. Typically found in evergreen forest or mixed-deciduous forest, but can also occur in urban parks during migration.

Eyebrowed Thrush *Turdus obscurus* 21–23cm

A medium-sized songbird that is often seen on the ground. Adult male has grey head with white eyebrow, rufous breast and flanks, and brown upperparts. Female and juvenile are duller and more poorly marked.

Where to see A common and widespread winter visitor and passage migrant. Typically seen in forested habitats but may occur in parks during migration. Usually seen in flocks visiting fruiting or flowering trees.

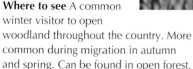

1st-win.

Asian Brown Flycatcher *Muscicapa dauurica* 12–14cm

A small brown flycatcher with a thin but broad-based bill. Rather nondescript. Identified from other brown flycatchers by the lack of any obvious streaking on the underparts and the brown moustachial stripe. Often confused with Taiga Flycatcher but note the brown tail that lacks any white at the base.

Where to see A common winter visitor to open woodland throughout the country. More common during migration in autumn and spring. Can be found in open forest, secondary forest and even urban parks. Remains still on exposed perches and flies out to snatch insects in midair.

Dark-sided Flycatcher *Muscicapa sibirica* 13–14cm

ssp. *cacabata*

ssp. *sibirica*

A small dull flycatcher with a very small bill and long wingtips. Darker and more greyish than other brown flycatchers. Underparts can be variable, with either streaks or plain grey wash on breast and flanks.

Where to see A common and widespread winter visitor and passage migrant in nearly all types of forest and even urban parks. Perches on exposed branches and flies out to catch insects in midair.

White-gorgeted Flycatcher *Anthipes monileger* 11.5–13cm

A very small brown flycatcher with large head and tiny bill. Face is slightly greyer than head and back, with a triangular white throat patch with black border.

Where to see
An uncommon resident of evergreen forest on high mountains in the north. Shy and secretive. Perches quietly on branches close to the ground in dark shady areas.

Taiga Flycatcher   *Ficedula albicilla* 11–12cm

br.

non-br.

A small brown bird with distinctive white patches at tail base. Often cocks and spreads tail when perched. Overall greyish-brown with white underparts and black tail. Small black bill and black legs. In breeding plumage, male has bright orange throat.

Where to see A common winter visitor throughout the region, except in the far south. Usually seen in urban parks, plantations, scrub and open forest.

Little Pied Flycatcher   *Ficedula westermanni* 10–11cm

♂

♀

A very small flycatcher with large head and tiny bill. Male has distinctive black-and-white plumage. Female is dull greyish-brown overall with more rufous-tinged tail and uppertail-coverts.

Where to see A common resident of hill evergreen forest and pine forest. Usually detected by the soft trilling call.

Flycatchers

Rufous-gorgeted Flycatcher *Ficedula strophiata* 13–14.5cm

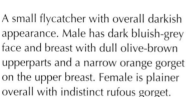

A small flycatcher with overall darkish appearance. Male has dark bluish-grey face and breast with dull olive-brown upperparts and a narrow orange gorget on the upper breast. Female is plainer overall with indistinct rufous gorget.

Tail is blackish with white base to the outer tail feathers.

Where to see A fairly common winter visitor to evergreen forest on high mountains in the north.

Yellow-rumped Flycatcher *Ficedula zanthopygia* 13–13.5cm

Male is readily identified by the bright yellow underparts and rump, black upperparts, and white eyebrow and wing patch. Female is dull olive-brown above and pale yellowish below, with a narrower yellow rump patch. Juvenile

male is very similar to the female but typically shows more white on the wings.

Where to see A fairly common passage migrant and winter visitor to lowland forest, parks and urban areas.

Large Niltava *Niltava grandis* 20–22cm

A large flycatcher with a relatively long tail that is often pumped and fanned. Male is dark bluish overall, with a brighter blue crown, neck patch and upperparts. Female is dull olive-brown overall with a small glossy blue patch on the neck. Females in the south have a blue wash on the crown.

Where to see A common resident of evergreen forest on high mountains. Typically perches quietly in shady areas and can be difficult to detect.

Rufous-bellied Niltava *Niltava sundara* 15–18cm

Male is strikingly beautiful, with bright orange underparts contrasting against the dark purplish-blue upperparts. Crown and shoulder are brighter blue than the rest of the plumage. Female is dull olive-brown overall with a small white patch on lower throat.

Where to see A fairly common winter visitor to evergreen forest on high mountains in the north and west. Usually perches in dense shrubs close to the ground.

Verditer Flycatcher *Eumyias thalassinus* 15–17cm

Male has distinctive bright turquoise plumage with a small black mask. Female is duller without a distinct black mask. Often confused with Pale Blue Flycatcher but has a much smaller bill, more greenish-tinged plumage and scaled undertail-coverts.

Where to see A fairly common resident of forested habitats throughout the country. Typically found in evergreen forest and secondary forest but might occur in urban parks in winter.

Hill Blue Flycatcher *Cyornis whitei* 14–15.5cm

Male is a classic blue flycatcher, with deep blue upperparts, rufous throat and breast that gradually grade into the white lower belly. Female has warm brown upperparts, with rufous-tinged tail and uppertail-coverts.

Where to see A common resident in hill evergreen forest except in the far north-east and far south. Also occurs in lowland and urban parks during winter.

Chinese Blue Flycatcher   *Cyornis glaucicomans* 14–15cm

Male is very similar to Blue-throated Flycatcher *Cyornis rubeculoides* but has darker blue upperparts with larger orange notch on the throat. Female is very difficult to differentiate from other blue flycatchers, especially female Hainan Blue Flycatcher *Cyornis hainanus*, but generally has paler and duller orange breast with pale buffish throat.

Where to see An uncommon winter visitor and passage migrant in lowland forests and even urban parks. Scarcer in the north and east.

Indochinese Blue Flycatcher   *Cyornis sumatrensis* 13.5–15.5cm

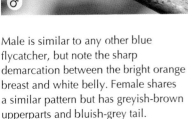

Male is similar to any other blue flycatcher, but note the sharp demarcation between the bright orange breast and white belly. Female shares a similar pattern but has greyish-brown upperparts and bluish-grey tail.

Where to see A common resident in deciduous forest, secondary forest, mangroves and plantations. Typically found in drier habitats at lower elevations than Hill Blue Flycatcher.

Oriental Magpie-robin *Copsychus saularis* 19–21cm

A terrestrial robin with strikingly bicoloured plumage. Male has glossy black head, breast, wings and tail, contrasting with white underparts. Bold white stripe across the wing. Female shares same pattern but has grey head and breast with dark sooty back. In flight shows prominent white wing patches and outer tail feathers.

Where to see A common bird in various habitats throughout the country. Adapts well to urban areas. Male is often seen singing from exposed perch like utility pole, wire and rooftop at dawn and dusk. Song is rich, complex and often mimics other birds.

White-rumped Shama *Copsychus malabaricus* 21–28cm

A beautiful robin with a very long tail and a conspicuous white rump patch. Male has dark glossy black head, breast, wings and tail contrasting with the deep rufous underparts. Female is duller and paler with shorter tail. Male gives series of melodic and extremely variable songs, often mimicking other birds.

Where to see A common bird in wooded habitats, from forest edge and secondary forest to hill evergreen forest. Much less common in the south where pressure from illegal songbird trade is much higher than elsewhere.

White-crowned Forktail *Enicurus leschenaulti* 25–28cm

A relatively large robin with black-and-white plumage. White forehead is constantly raised and lowered while feeding. Tail is black and deeply forked with bold white tips. Juvenile has completely blackish-brown head and breast. Population in the south is smaller with a shorter tail.

Where to see A fairly common resident in hill evergreen forest in the north, west and north-east. Scarce and occurs only in lowland forest in the south.

Slaty-backed Forktail *Enicurus schistaceus* 22–25cm

A medium-sized robin with a long deeply forked tail that is often pumped while walking and running along rocky streams. Easily distinguished from other forktails by the grey crown and back.

Where to see A fairly common resident in hill evergreen forest with streams. Scarce and very local in the south. Typically skittish and usually seen flying away along a stream.

Blue Whistling-thrush *Myophonus caeruleus* 29–35cm

migratory

resident

A large thrush-like bird with overall dark purplish-blue plumage. Resident populations have bright yellow bill, while the most widespread migratory race has an all-black bill. Often pumps and fans the tail when perched.

Where to see Fairly common in various forested habitats and limestone hills, particularly with forest streams. Very active at dawn and often seen along roads before sunrise.

Blue Rock-thrush *Monticola solitarius* 20–23cm

♂ br.

♂ non-br.

A medium-sized songbird. Male is greyish-blue overall with buffish scales throughout in non-breeding plumage. Female is slightly browner overall with more heavily mottled underparts. Males of the migratory race *philippensis* have a chestnut belly and undertail-coverts.

Where to see A fairly common winter visitor throughout the country, and a resident in the south. Typically found in open wooded habitats, but the resident race can occur in coastal areas. Often seen on exposed perches.

Chestnut-bellied Rock-thrush *Monticola rufiventris* 21–23cm

Male is a beautiful bird with dark blue head and upperparts, and rich chestnut underparts. Female is dull greyish-brown overall with buff spots on the face and throat, and heavily scaled underparts.

Where to see An uncommon resident of evergreen forest and pine forest on high mountains in the north. Perches motionlessly on exposed treetops.

White-tailed Robin *Myiomela leucura* 17–19cm

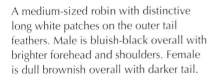

A medium-sized robin with distinctive long white patches on the outer tail feathers. Male is bluish-black overall with brighter forehead and shoulders. Female is dull brownish overall with darker tail.

Where to see A fairly common resident of evergreen forest on high mountains in the north, west and north-east. Shy and secretive. Rarely strays from the dark forest undergrowth.

White-capped Redstart *Phoenicurus leucocephalus* 18–19cm

An unmistakable bird of three colours. The head, breast, wings and tail tip are black, with contrasting red underparts, rump and tail, and a long and narrow white cap.

Where to see An uncommon winter visitor to forest streams and waterfalls in the north. Perches on rocks and tree trunks, with the tail held constantly cocked.

Siberian Blue Robin *Larvivora cyane* 13–14cm

A small robin with a very short and square-ended tail. Male is unmistakable, with blue upperparts contrasting strongly against the white underparts. Female is dull olive-brown overall with a greyish-blue tail, and light brownish scales on the breast. Frequently quivers the tail while feeding on or near the ground.

Where to see A fairly common and widespread winter visitor to forested habitats. Typically found in evergreen forest but can also occur in urban parks during migration.

Siberian Rubythroat *Calliope calliope* 14–16cm

A medium-sized robin with overall brown plumage and a white eyebrow. Male has bright red throat bordered with bold white moustachial stripes. Female has white throat. Tail is brown without any white patches. Forages on or close to the ground. Frequently cocks and holds the tail upright while perched.

Where to see A fairly common winter visitor to wetlands, grasslands and any shrubby habitats in lowlands and on mountains. More abundant in the north and absent from the south.

Bluethroat *Luscinia svecica* 13–15cm

A sandy-brown, terrestrial robin. Tail has conspicuous orange patches near base typically visible in flight while landing. Male has blue, black and rufous patches on the throat and breast, while female usually has only black streaks.

Where to see A fairly common winter visitor to grasslands and cultivated places, except in the south where it is rare and irregular. Runs on open ground with the tail constantly cocked or raised.

Amur Stonechat *Saxicola stejnegeri* 12.5cm

A small chat with a large head and short tail. Male in breeding plumage has black head, wings and tail, with large white patches on the neck, shoulder and rump. Rufous underparts fade into the white undertail-coverts. Female is much duller and plainer with overall buffish-brown plumage. Male in non-breeding plumage has buffy scales over the upperparts.

Where to see A common winter visitor except in the far south. Typically found in open grassland, wetlands, cultivated areas and forest clearings. Assumes exposed perches looking for prey on the ground.

Pied Bushchat *Saxicola caprata* 13–14cm

Male is easily identified by the overall black plumage with contrasting white undertail-coverts and wing patch. Female can be easily confused with other chats but note the overall dark brownish plumage and rufous rump patch.

Where to see A fairly common resident in the north and north-east. Typically found in dry and open habitats such as dry grassland, cultivation and forest clearings. Uses exposed perches, looking for prey on the ground.

Grey Bushchat *Saxicola ferreus* 14–15cm

A small chat with a large head and relatively long tail. Male is grey overall with a bold black mask, white eyebrow and dark-streaked back. Female has overall rufous-brown plumage with paler underparts and a white eyebrow.

Where to see A common resident of grassland, open forest and forest clearings on high mountains in the north. Can be found in lowlands during winter and sometimes occurs in central Thailand.

Himalayan Shortwing *Brachypteryx cruralis* 13cm

A small robin with a large head, long legs and short tail. Male is readily identified by the overall dark bluish plumage with prominent white eyebrow. Female is warm brown overall with a slightly more rufous eyebrow.

Where to see An uncommon or locally common resident of evergreen forest on high mountains in the north. Can be difficult to detect while foraging on the dark forest floor.

Greater Green Leafbird *Chloropsis sonnerati* 18–21cm

An overall green leafbird with a relatively large bill. Male has black face with a small blue moustachial stripe. Female lacks any black on the head but has yellow throat and eye-ring instead.

Where to see A scarce and declining bird of evergreen forest in the south and south-west. Has seriously declined due to illegal songbird trade. Now found only in well-protected forests.

Golden-fronted Leafbird *Chloropsis aurifrons* 17–19cm

A medium-sized songbird with overall green plumage. Adult has bright orange forehead and black face with dark blue throat. Populations in the north and north-east have a yellow border around the black facial patch. Females in the south-west have less black on the face than males.

Where to see A fairly common bird of deciduous forest, secondary forest and forest edge. Usually visits flowering and fruiting trees, especially Jamaica Cherry (*Muntingia calabura*).

Blue-winged Leafbird *Chloropsis cochinchinensis* 16.5–18.5cm

Overall bright yellowish-green with blue wing panel and tail. Male has golden-yellow head with black face and a small blue moustachial stripe. Female lacks any black on the face.

Where to see A fairly common resident of forested habitats including evergreen forest, mixed-deciduous forest and secondary forest. Much scarcer in the south due to the illegal songbird trade.

Orange-bellied Leafbird *Chloropsis hardwickii* 17–19.8cm

A vividly coloured songbird with bright green upperparts and an orange belly. Male has a large black patch on the face and breast, with a blue throat, wing panel and tail. Female has an all-green head and breast, and a pale blue patch on the throat.

Where to see A fairly common resident in evergreen forest in northern, western and far north-eastern Thailand. Typically found on high mountains but sometimes descends to foothills.

Yellow-breasted Flowerpecker *Prionochilus maculatus* 10cm

A tiny bird with short thick bill and short tail. Upperparts are olive-brown with yellow underparts. Throat is white with distinct moustachial stripes. Has bold olive-brown stripes on the breast and flanks. Male has bright orange patch on the crown.

Where to see A common resident of lowland forest, secondary forest and plantations in the south. Usually seen visiting fruiting trees or joining mixed-species flocks.

Orange-bellied Flowerpecker *Dicaeum trigonostigma* 8–9cm

A tiny and brightly coloured bird. Male has bluish-grey head, breast, wings and tail with bright orange back and belly. Female is olive-brown overall with more yellowish underparts. Extremely fast and vocal, giving a series of very high-pitched calls.

Where to see A common resident in evergreen forest, secondary forest, forest edge and plantations in the south and west. Frequently joins mixed-species flocks and visits fruiting trees.

Plain Flowerpecker *Dicaeum minullum* 7.5–8.5cm

A tiny and nondescript bird. Olive-brown overall with black beady eyes and a pale grey bill. Completely lacks any bright colours. Best separated from females of other flowerpeckers, especially Fire-breasted (*Dicaeum ignipectus*) and Scarlet-backed Flowerpeckers, by the lack of contrasting pattern on the breast-sides and absence of a bright red patch on the rump.

Where to see A common resident in forested habitats from evergreen forest to forest edge and plantations. Usually seen at fruiting or flowering trees.

Scarlet-backed Flowerpecker *Dicaeum cruentatum* 7–9cm

A tiny and extremely active bird. Male has bright red crown to rump bordered by glossy black face, wings and flanks, contrasting with the white underparts. Female is greyish-brown overall with a bright red patch on the rump. Gives repetitive metallic clicking sounds and extremely high-pitched songs.

Where to see A common bird in urban areas throughout the country. Often seen in parks, plantations, forest edge and secondary forest in the lowlands. Visits flowering and fruiting trees, especially mistletoes and *Muntingia calabura*.

Yellow-vented Flowerpecker *Dicaeum chrysorrheum* 9–10cm

As the name implies, a flowerpecker with distinctive yellow undertail-coverts. Underparts are white with long dark brownish streaks, while the upperparts are plain olive-brown. Identified from the similar Yellow-breasted Flowerpecker by having no yellow on throat and breast, and more well-defined streaks on the underparts.

Where to see A common flowerpecker of forested habitats from evergreen forest and mixed-deciduous forest to secondary forest and forest edge.

Little Spiderhunter *Arachnothera longirostra* 13.3–16cm

A small spiderhunter with a very long and narrow bill. Olive upperparts contrast with the white throat and bright yellow belly. Active and vocal. Gives loud harsh calls both while feeding and flying.

Where to see A common bird in various types of forested habitats including evergreen forest, secondary forest and plantations. Frequently seen feeding on the nectar of banana flowers.

Grey-breasted Spiderhunter *Arachnothera modesta* 17–18cm

A dull spiderhunter with olive upperparts and greyish underparts. Breast is slightly streaked when seen at close range. Bill is long and downcurved like other spiderhunters. Legs and feet are pale pinkish. Outer tail feathers have broad pale tips that are only visible when the tail is spread.

Where to see A common resident of lowland forest, foothills and plantations in the south. Usually visits flowering banana trees and joins mixed-species flocks.

Streaked Spiderhunter *Arachnothera magna* 17–20.5cm

A chunky spiderhunter with overall heavily streaked plumage. Upperparts are greenish-yellow contrasting with the whitish underparts. Has long and narrow black streaks throughout the body. Bill is long and downcurved. The feet are bright orange.

Where to see A common resident of hill evergreen forest in the north, west and far south. Usually seen visiting flowering banana trees or joining mixed-species flocks.

Brown-throated Sunbird *Anthreptes malacensis* 12–13.5cm

A small and active bird with a long, pointed bill. Male is extremely colourful with yellow underparts and various iridescent colours on the head and back. Wing-coverts and throat are chestnut-brown. Female looks completely different, with overall plain yellowish underparts and olive-brown upperparts.

Where to see A common garden bird that is found in parks, plantations, mangrove and secondary forest. Usually seen at flowering trees. Less common and more local in the north and north-east.

Ornate Sunbird *Cinnyris ornatus* 10–11.4cm

A tiny and very active bird with overall yellowish plumage. Olive-brown upperparts contrast with the bright yellow underparts in both sexes. Male has dark glossy blue neck and breast with a broad dark chestnut breast-band. Builds a sack-shaped nest suspended from the tip of a branch or various human-made objects.

Where to see Very common in gardens, parks, plantations and forest edge throughout the country. Usually seen at flowering trees where it uses its long decurved bill to feed on nectar.

Purple Sunbird *Cinnyris asiaticus* 10–11cm

A small sunbird with a short bill and tail. Male is dark, glossy purplish-blue in breeding plumage with a narrow dark chestnut breast-band. Female is very similar to Ornate Sunbird but has slightly greyer underparts. Eclipse male is similar to female but has a narrow dark line in the middle of throat and breast, with a small glossy blue shoulder patch.

Where to see A fairly common resident of deciduous forest, secondary forest, cultivation and parks in the north, west and north-east. Often seen visiting flowering trees.

Crimson Sunbird *Aethopyga siparaja* 11–12cm (male), 10cm (female)

Male is a striking small bird with bright red head, breast and back, dull greyish underparts, and a glossy green or bluish tail. Plumage varies across the country, with the population in the far north having the longest tail and those in the far south the darkest plumage. Female is dull olive-brown overall.

Where to see A fairly common resident in evergreen forest, secondary forest and mixed-deciduous forest. Typically found in lowlands.

Black-throated Sunbird   *Aethopyga saturata* 14–15cm (male), 10cm (female)

Male is a small sunbird with a very long glossy blue tail. Head and breast are blackish with glossy blue crown and throat. Wings are black with dark maroon mantle. Underparts are pale yellowish with faint reddish wash on the breast. Female is olive-brown overall with a short tail and distinctive lemon rump patch.

Where to see A fairly common resident in evergreen forest on high mountains. Usually seen visiting flowering trees like other sunbirds.

Mrs. Gould's Sunbird   *Aethopyga gouldiae* 14–15cm (male), 10cm (female)

Male is an extremely colourful bird with bright scarlet breast, yellow belly and a very long glossy blue tail. Head is red with patches of iridescent blue on the crown and throat. Female is rather nondescript except for the pale lemon rump patch.

Where to see A common winter visitor to evergreen forest on high mountains in the north, west and north-east. Usually seen visiting blooming flowers.

Green-tailed Sunbird   *Aethopyga nipalensis* 14–15cm

Male is distinctive with metallic green head and tail. Underparts are bright yellow with olive wings and a maroon back. The population at Doi Inthanon has a bright scarlet wash on the breast. Female is duller olive-brown overall with greyer forehead.

Where to see A very local species but is common where found. Only known from the summits of several high mountains in Chiang Mai, Tak and Nakhon Si Thammarat.

House Sparrow   *Passer domesticus* 14–16.5cm

A chunky sparrow with sexually dimorphic plumage. Male has a grey crown, chestnut crescent patch behind the large white cheek, and a large black patch on throat and breast. Female is dull greyish-brown overall with a heavily streaked back.

Where to see A common and widespread bird except in the far south. Mostly found in farmland and urban areas. Usually seen in flocks, which can be extremely large in winter, or mixing with other seed-eating species.

Plain-backed Sparrow *Passer flaveolus* 13.5–15cm

A beautiful sparrow with sexually dimorphic plumage. Male has yellowish underparts with a greyish-green crown and rump. Chestnut eye-stripe and plain chestnut back without any dark streaking as in other sparrows. Black lores and black small bib. Female is yellowish-brown overall with plain brown back.

Where to see A fairly common sparrow of open habitats such as grassland, cultivation, forest edge and urban parks. Formerly much more abundant and widespread but has gradually declined again, probably due to nest competition with House Sparrows.

Eurasian Tree Sparrow *Passer montanus* 14–15cm

One of the most common and widespread birds in Thailand. Small with large, round head and short, cone-shaped bill. Differs from other sparrows by having a prominent black patch on the lower cheek. Chestnut cap with small black bib. The sexes are similar, unlike other sparrows.

Where to see Highly adaptable. Can be found in farmland and urban areas throughout the country. Usually seen near humans where it feeds on food scraps and nests in buildings. Hops on the ground looking for seeds and small insects. Often seen in large flocks where food is abundant.

Asian Golden Weaver   *Ploceus hypoxanthus*   15cm

A chunky weaver with a short stout bill. Female and non-breeding male have buffish-brown plumage with streaked upperparts. Male moults into a bright golden-yellow plumage with a black mask when breeding. Builds ball-shaped nests on low vegetation near water.

Where to see Common and widespread in rice fields and wetlands throughout the central plains. More local and less numerous elsewhere. Usually seen in flocks, often mixed with other seed-eating species.

Baya Weaver   *Ploceus philippinus*   15cm

Very similar to Asian Golden Weaver in non-breeding plumage but has thinner and more pointed bill. Male has bright golden-yellow crown with blackish mask in breeding plumage. Builds sack-shaped nests with long entrance tubes, suspended from tall trees.

Where to see The most abundant and widespread weaver in Thailand. Typically found in rice fields, wetlands and cultivated areas. Often in big flocks mixed with other seed-eating species.

Streaked Weaver *Ploceus manyar* 15cm

Similar to Baya Weaver but has distinct black streaks on breast and flanks. Easily told from other weavers in non-breeding plumage by the bright yellow neck patch. Male in breeding plumage has blackish face and throat, with bright yellow crown.

Where to see A common resident in wetlands and rice fields in central and western Thailand. Scarce and local in the north and north-east.

Java Sparrow *Padda oryzivora* 14–17cm

A bulky sparrow-like bird with unmistakable plumage. Overall pale grey with pinkish belly, black head, white cheeks and a large pinkish bill. Juvenile is dull brownish-grey overall with paler cheeks.

Where to see An introduced species that is locally abundant in northern Bangkok. Often seen in large flocks while roosting and feeding in rice fields.

Red Avadavat   *Amandava amandava*   9.5–10cm

A tiny munia with a bright red bill. Male is overall bright red, with small white spots in the breeding plumage. Female and non-breeding male have overall brown plumage with a bright red rump patch. Males in northernmost Thailand have a pale yellowish belly in breeding plumage.

Where to see A fairly common resident of grasslands, wetlands and rice fields except in the south. Gregarious and vocal. Typically seen in flocks mixing with other munias and weavers.

Scaly-breasted Munia   *Lonchura punctulata*   12–12.5cm

A small brown bird with a stout cone-shaped bill. Adult has dark earth-brown upperparts and white underparts with brown scales on the breast and flanks. Juvenile is plain buffish-brown overall. Feeds mainly on grass and rice seeds. Usually seen in flocks that sometimes consort with other seed-eating species.

Where to see A very common resident of open habitats throughout the country. Most abundant in rice fields where large flocks are often seen during the harvesting season. Also common in villages and urban areas such as parks.

Chestnut Munia *Lonchura atricapilla* 11–12cm

Adult is distinctive with overall dark chestnut plumage and a contrasting black head. Juvenile is plain buffish-brown overall with a slightly darker head. Bill is lead-grey both in the adult and juvenile. Usually seen in flocks mixing with other seed-eating species.

Where to see A fairly common resident of grasslands, wetlands and rice fields in central, southern and north-eastern Thailand. Scarce and local in the north.

White-rumped Munia *Lonchura striata* 11–12cm

A small dark munia with whitish underparts. At close range, pale brownish scales on the underparts are visible. Has a distinctive white rump patch that is best seen in flight. Juvenile is duller and plainer overall.

Where to see Common and widespread in various habitat types. Typically found in rice fields, cultivation, urban parks and even open forest. Often seen in flocks, sometimes mixed with other munias and weavers.

Forest Wagtail *Dendronanthus indicus* 16–18cm

An unusual wagtail with olive-brown upperparts and white underparts. Easily distinguished from other pipits and wagtails by the bold black bands across the breast and wings. Wags tail sideways while walking or perched.

Where to see A fairly common passage migrant and winter visitor throughout the country. Usually found in wooded habitats but also occurs in urban parks during migration.

Grey Wagtail *Motacilla cinerea* 17–20cm

Slim with a long and narrow tail that is constantly pumped. Typically seen in non-breeding plumage, with grey back, white throat and yellow underparts. Has a large black throat patch in breeding plumage. Typically seen walking on open ground or when flushed from roads.

Where to see A common winter visitor to many kinds of habitats throughout the country. Typically found in forested areas but also seen in rice fields and wetlands.

non-br.

Wagtails

Citrine Wagtail *Motacilla citreola* 16.5–20cm

In non-breeding plumage, separated from other wagtails by the combination of greyish crown and back, white underparts and bright yellow face. Very distinctive in breeding plumage, with bright yellow head and underparts contrasting with the grey upperparts.

Where to see A fairly common winter visitor to rice fields and wetlands in the north. Scarcer and less numerous elsewhere.

Eastern Yellow Wagtail *Motacilla tschutschensis* 16.5–18cm

A beautiful wagtail with bright yellow underparts, grey head and green back. Many subspecies occur in the region. The subspecies differ by head colour and the extent (or lack) of white eyebrow. Juvenile has similar pattern to the adult but lacks any bright colour in the plumage.

Where to see A common and widespread winter visitor to wetlands and rice fields. Can be found in both freshwater and coastal wetlands.

White Wagtail   *Motacilla alba* 16.5–18cm

Overall a whitish wagtail, as its name implies, but plumage can be extremely variable depending on the subspecies. The most common and widespread subspecies, *M. a. leucopsis*, has all-white face with a black breast patch, and black back in the male (grey in the female). Other subspecies mainly differ by the head pattern and colour of the back.

Where to see A common winter visitor to northern Thailand. Less common southward, and rare in the south. Typically found in rice fields and wetlands.

Olive-backed Pipit   *Anthus hodgsoni* 15–17cm

A small pipit with olive-brown upperparts and white underparts with pale buffish wash on the face and breast. Has bold black streaks on the underparts and a bold facial pattern. Tail is rather short with white outer tail feathers and is frequently pumped.

Where to see A common and widespread winter visitor to various open habitats except in the south. Typically found in open forest, parks, plantations and sometimes grasslands. Feeds mainly on the ground but flies up into trees when disturbed.

Richard's Pipit *Anthus richardi* 17–18cm

A large pipit with a relatively long tail compared to other species. Overall warm brown with streaked crown, breast and back. Very similar to Paddyfield Pipit but has different flight calls, larger bill, paler lores and longer tail. Stands upright while foraging on the ground.

Where to see A common and widespread winter visitor to open grassland and cultivation. Much scarcer in the south. Typically seen singly or in small loose flocks with other pipits and wagtails.

Paddyfield Pipit *Anthus rufulus* 15–16cm

juv.

A small terrestrial bird with a fine bill and long tail. Usually appears quite slender. Stands upright while foraging on the ground. Overall buffish-brown with streaked crown, breast and back. Dark loral stripe in front of the eye. Legs are relatively long with unusually long hind toes.

Where to see The only common resident pipit in the region. Found in various open habitats such as grassland, farmland and open lawns. Feeds primarily on the ground but sings from exposed perches.

Common Rosefinch *Carpodacus erythrinus* 13–15cm

A small songbird with a heavy cone-shaped bill. Male has pinkish-red head, throat and breast, and browner upperparts. Female is olive-brown overall with slightly streaked underparts and bold whitish wing-bars.

Where to see A fairly common winter visitor to grassland and open forest in the north and north-east. Typically found in the mountains but may also occur in lowlands.

♀ ♂

Yellow-breasted Bunting *Emberiza aureola* 14–15.5cm

♂ br.

♂ non-br.

Globally Critically Endangered. Has bright yellow throat and underparts with streaked brown head and upperparts in non-breeding plumage. Male in breeding plumage has black head, dark chestnut upperparts and a chestnut breast-band.

Where to see Scarce or locally common winter visitor to rice fields, reedbeds and marshes. Roosts in large flocks with other seed-eating species. Rare and irregular in the south.

FURTHER READING AND RESOURCES

Birds of Thailand by Uthai Treesucon and Wich'yanan Limparungpatthanakij (2018, Lynx Edicions)

Field Guide to the Birds of South-East Asia by Craig Robson (2018, Helm)

A Naturalist's Guide to the Birds of Thailand by Philip D. Round (2018, John Beaufoy)

eBird.org (ebird.org/region/TH)

The Clements Checklist of Birds of the World (birds.cornell.edu/clementschecklist)

Bird Conservation Society of Thailand (bcst.or.th)

Acknowledgements

I would like to thank my parents, Kijja and Panthip Jearwattanakanok, for always supporting my passion in birdwatching and arts. I am grateful to be able to start pursuing my dreams at such a young age. A special thanks to Rungsrit Kanjanavanit, the chair of Lanna Bird Club, who inspired me and countless numbers of people around Thailand both as a naturalist and a wildlife artist. I would also like to extend my thanks to everyone who has been involved in bird conservation in Thailand especially my colleagues at the Bird Conservation Society of Thailand who have worked tirelessly to make Thailand a better place for birds and nature. Lastly, I would really like to thank my publisher, Jim Martin, for approaching me to undertake this project. This book is certainly another milestone for me. I am more than grateful to him for offering me the opportunity. Thank you also to my editors, Laura Browning-Brant and Jenny Campbell, for their assistance with the manuscript, format and layout.